D1328123

*Publications of the*

CENTRE FOR REFORMATION AND RENAISSANCE STUDIES

Renaissance and Reformation Texts in Translation, 5

SERIES EDITOR    John McClelland

# A Reformation Debate:
# Karlstadt, Emser, and Eck on Sacred Images
# Three Treatises in Translation

Translated, with an introduction and notes, by
Bryan D. Mangrum and Giuseppe Scavizzi
Second edition, revised

Toronto
Centre for Reformation and Renaissance Studies
1998

**Canadian Cataloguing in Publication Data**

Main entry under title:

A Reformation Debate: Karlstadt, Emser, and Eck on Sacred Images
(Renaissance and Reformation Texts in Translation; 5)
2nd ed. rev.

Translation of: Von Abtuhung der Bylder; Das Man der heyligen Bilder in der
     Kirchen nit Abthon, noch unehren soll und das sie in der Schrifft
     nyndert verbotten seyn; De non tollendis Christi et sanctorum
     imaginibus.

Contents: On the removal of images / Andreas Karlstadt. – That one should
     not remove images of the saints from the churches nor dishonour them
     and that they are not forbidden in scripture / Hieronymus Emser. – On
     not removing images of Christ and the saints / Johannes Eck.

ISBN 0-9697512-7-3

     1. Idols and images – Worship – Controversial literature. 2. Iconoclasm
– Controversial literature. 3. Catholic Church – Doctrines.  I. Mangrum,
Bryan D.  II. Scavizzi, Giuseppe.  III. Karlstadt, Andreas Rudolff-Bodenstein
von, ca. 1480–1541 On the removal of images.  IV. Emser, Hieronymus,
1478–1527 That one should not remove images of the saints from the
churches nor dishonour them and that they are not forbidden in scripture.
V. Eck, Johann, 1486–1543 On not removing images of Christ and the saints.
VI. Victoria University (Toronto, Ontario). Centre for Reformation and
Renaissance Studies.  VII. Title.  VIII. Series.

BR355.135K37 1998 246'.5 C91-090016-7

For orders or information on the series:
     Centre for Reformation and Renaissance Studies
     Victoria University in the University of Toronto
     Toronto, Canada, M5S 1K7
     Tel: (416) 585-4484  Fax: (416) 585-4579

Typeset by Becker Associates

Cover Illustration: *Crucifixion* from Martin Luther, *Das dise Wort Christi ...
noch feststehn wieder die Schwermergeister* (Wittemberg, 1589)

# Contents

# *Preface*

The treatise by Andreas Karlstadt, *Von Abtuhung der Bylder*, was published in Wittenberg in January 1522. It is composed of two distinct sections, the first on the removal of images, the second on the need to discourage begging; only the first section of the treatise has been translated here. The translation has been based on the reprint made by H. Lietzmann (Kleine Texte für theologische und philologische Vorlesungen und Übungen, no. 74. Bonn, 1911; the text was also reprinted in *Flugschriften der frühen Reformationsbewegung* (1518–24); see Laube in the Select Bibliography), which can be consulted for information and bibliography (for more information on the treatise see R. J. Sider, *Andreas Bodenstein von Karlstadt,* 167ff). The title page of the book reads:

> Von abtuhung der Bylder/ | Vnd das keyn Betdler | vnther
> den Chri= | sten seyn soll. | [fig.] | Carolstatt. in der Christlichê
> | statt Wittenberg
> [a colophon specifies that the book was printed by Nyckell
> Schyrlentz and that the printing was completed on 27 January]

The treatise by Hieronymus Emser, *Das man der heyligen bilder in der kirchen nit abthon*, was published in Dresden. In his dedication Emser gives the date of 2 April 1522. Our translation is based on the copy in the Bayerische Staatsbibliothek in Munich. For date, edition, and bibliography see H. Smolinsky, "Reformation und Bildersturm," 429. The title page of the book reads:

> Das man der heyli | gê bilder yn den kirchê nit abthon / noch |
> unehren soll / Und das sie yn der | schrifft nyndert verbottê
> seyn. | Hieronymus Emser. | [fig. an heraldic device consisting
> of a plumed helmet and shield, each bearing a horned ram's
> head; an inset plaque identifies the device as the "ARMA HIE |
> RONYMI | EMSER."] |
> [No imprint]

The treatise by Johannes Eck, *De non tollendis Christi et sanctorum imaginibus*, was published in more than one edition in 1522–23, and again in 1531 (on these editions and dates of publication see J. Metzler in *Corpus Catholicorum*, vol. 16 (Münster, 1930), lxxxvi; E. Iserloh, "Die Verteidigung," 76; and here Introduction, note 31). Our translation has been based on the copy also in the Bayerische Staatsbibliothek of Munich (Ingolstadt, 1523) but the other early edition published in Ingolstadt in 1522 has also been consulted (one copy of the latter edition is at St Michael's College Library, University of Toronto). The title page of the 1523 edition reads:

> De non tollêdis | Christi & sanctorum Imaginibus: contra |
> haeresim Faelicianam sub Carolo magno | damnatam: & iam
> sub Carolo .V. renascê | tem decisio. | [fig. the Trinity]
> [a colophon indicates that the printing was completed on
> 3 March 1523]

*  *  *  *  *

The paragraphing in Karlstadt and Emser has been respected, while that in Eck has been supplied by the translators due to the fact that Eck's chapters are uninterrupted paragraphs. Punctuation has been modernized. In so far as possible, we have tried to preserve the style of the original texts, but it has, of course, been necessary to break up and simplify long, convoluted sentences, or at times to assemble exceedingly short ones. All three texts were obviously written in the heat of the controversy, and their literary style is not always very polished; from this point of view the translation from Karlstadt has been particularly difficult, since his prose has at times the abrupt cadences and ellipses of oral speech. Parentheses are part of the original documents, while square brackets are ours. We have elected not to indicate every instance in which an additional word missing in the original text but clearly understood has been supplied, and we also have avoided making a note of all the corruptions of the texts (especially numerous in Eck's treatise); we have reported however all the cases in which either the distraction of the writers or the corruptions of the text could lead to different interpretations.

Given the manner of writing of many sixteenth-century theologians, who constantly took inspiration from the Scriptures but rarely quoted with precision from their source, we have not given *all* biblical references (extremely numerous in Karlstadt's text, for which the reader can in any case refer to Lietzmann's notes). Also, scriptural paraphrases and other references have been translated from the texts themselves; the (rare) verbatim quotations from the Vulgate have been rendered according to the King James version. In no case have quotation marks been used.

References to canon and civil law have been left as given in the texts. A few references to important works of the Fathers have also been left as given in the text, for the information provided by the authors is sufficient to trace the quotation.

In editing and translating these texts we have received much help from friends and colleagues to whom we would like here to express our gratitude. Professor Karl Denner of McMaster University was kind enough to review a first draft of the Karlstadt text. Professors John Grant and Wolfgang Hempel of the University of Toronto were encouraging and made many useful suggestions, as did the anonymous readers who vetted our manuscripts at various stages of their development. We owe a special measure of thanks to Donald Smith of Atticus Books in Toronto, whose linguistic skills and philological knowledge played no small role in helping us bring our task to a conclusion. If weaknesses and errors are still to be found in the work, the responsibility is exclusively ours. Finally, we would like to thank Professor John McClelland, Professor Konrad Eisen-bichler, Dr Michael Milway, and Mary Watt of the CRRS for their help and patience in guiding our text through the process of publication.

# Introduction

## The Debate on Images
## at the Beginning of the Reformation:
## Karlstadt, Emser, and Eck

That the widespread iconoclasm of the Reformation represented a necessary step for the development of modern Christianity, and one could say also of Western culture, is an unquestioned and unquestionable assumption. Modern studies, following the pioneering work of scholars like Huizinga and Coulton,[1] have pointed out that the devotion of the late Middle Ages had become more and more inclined to associate religion with the visual and the tactile, and had expanded enormously that part of the ritual which the theologians called *coeremonialia*. Many of the devotions common at the time were related to visible objects, and among them a very prominent place was occupied by the cult of images. Images were the goal of long pilgrimages, brought about miracles, were an integral part of a series of practices perceived by most people as ways to achieve salvation; and because they embodied some special qualities which could be termed sacred (whatever the meaning that then, or today, could be given to this word), images were venerated or even worshipped.[2] It might be noted in fact that, although it was generally stated that images only deserved *dulia*, a lesser form of veneration, according to Thomas Aquinas images deserved the same honour as the 'prototype' (or subject represented), so that for example the crucifix could be venerated with the same honour given to Christ, that is *latria*.[3]

---

[1] J. Huizinga, *The Waning of the Middle Ages* (London: Arnold, 1924), and G.G. Coulton, *Art and the Reformation*.

[2] On the distinction between the various degrees of honour, see below, note 17.

[3] T. Aquinas, *Summa theologiae*, Pt. III, art. 1–4.

A great variety of different beliefs was especially associated with images. For instance, someone who looked upon and prayed to an image of St Christopher was assured that he would not die in mortal sin during the day; for this reason images of this saint multiplied in the churches, in the streets, and in private houses. The crucifix was believed to have the power of driving away the Devil, and therefore a dying man, fearing that the Devil would take advantage of his weakness to steal his soul, would look upon, touch, and kiss the image of Christ on the cross; the beneficial power of the cross was witnessed by copious miracles and by many examples of conversion, as we can see in several stories narrated in the *Golden Legend*. The power of the many patron saints seemed to be present in a special way in their images, which were therefore used in a protective function on the gates of cities, on banners and other insignia. The image seemed to grant favours or even speak to the worshipper. St Bernard, St Thomas Aquinas, and many other saints and common people had experienced such things. Images, in other words, took on what some modern sociologists of religion would call a para-sacramentary quality; a quality, that is, which was conferred upon them by an act of consecration and which transformed them into vehicles of divine power. During the sixteenth century, through the work of both the Reformation and the Counter-Reformation, such beliefs were attacked or re-evaluated, and actually most of them faded away or were transformed; the significance of the so-called externals diminished, while, correspondingly, the sacraments became more important. However, there is no doubt that before the Reformation started in 1517 many superstitions arose from the cult of images.[4]

---

[4] On devotion in the late Middle Ages, see the recent review of problems and bibliography in Christensen, *Art and the Reformation*, 13–23, and Eire, *The War Against the Idols*, 8–27. On 'agic' in the Middle Ages, see K. Thomas, *Religion and the Decline of Magic* (Harmondsworth: Penguin, 1973); D. Freedberg, *Iconoclasts and Their Motives* (Maarsen: Schwarz, 1985) rejects the notion that the word magic should be used in relation to the cult of images in the late Middle Ages. As the veneration of images is related to the veneration of the saints and their relics, the geography of the areas in Europe where these cults flourished with greater intensity was probably related to factors deeply seated in the conscience of common people during the Middle Ages, as demonstrated by the challenging perspective offered by Lionel Rothkrug in his *Religious Practices and Collective*

Images were also associated with a variety of social 'evils.' As vehicles for the diffusion of the cult of the saints they reinforced the already overwhelming power of the clergy, not only because the saints were an expression of the ecclesiastical world, but because images could be and frequently were used by the hierarchy to increase its political and theological leverage, either by controlling their use in specific circumstances or by arranging their distribution according to the demands of certain orders or clerical sectors. The use of images also reinforced the dual nature of the late medieval Church (that is the distinction between clergy and laity), which represented a major social problem, because while they were originally and widely justified as a way of educating the illiterate about religious matters (they were the so-called Bible of the illiterate), over the centuries images had come in fact to confine and limit the spiritual life of the lower classes and of the laity in general.

It was inevitable that the elimination of those visual aids which led people to "superstition and idolatry" (to adopt a common expression of sixteenth-century Reformers) would be one of the chief goals of the Reformation. Indeed, in many parts of Europe the removal of religious pictures and statues from churches was witnessed with a great sense of relief. The reform of images, started by Karlstadt in Wittenberg, became a standard element of Reformation policy in several Swiss cities, starting in Zurich in 1523 where just a few months after the controversy in Wittenberg Zwingli persuaded the city council to agree to the removal of images from churches.[5] The battle against images continued unabated in Switzerland during the '30s and '40s. There is almost no need to remind the reader that among second generation Reformers Calvin made opposition to idols one of the principal elements of his overall policy. Partly because images were such a visible part of 'popish' superstitious practices, but certainly also for purely doctrinal reasons, Calvin unleashed in the

---

Perceptions. Hidden Homologies in the Renaissance and Reformation (Univ. of Waterloo, Ont., 1980). On medieval movements against images, see also Emser below, note 1.

For the art historian, a particularly good guide to the use of images and popular piety in the late 15th and early 16th centuries is to be found in Baxandall, *The Limewood Sculptors*, 50–93.

[5] On Zwingli, see Garside, *Zwingli and the Arts*.

'50s and '60s a (sometimes by proxy) war on images which created turbulence and intensified the confrontation with his opponents in various parts of Europe, particularly in France and the Low Countries.[6]

Many Calvinists took up the pen to fight images in Switzerland, France, and the Low Countries, among them Marnix de Saint Aldegonde and Beza.[7] But it was not only in the part of Europe dominated by Swiss theology that the war on images raged. In England a whole generation of Reformers focused their energy on fighting the superstitions connected with images. By the end of the sixteenth century, most of Reformed Europe had pretty well rid itself of religious images. Even Protestant Germany, where Luther had taken a moderate position on the issue and actually favoured the development of a new iconography, stopped producing religious art.[8]

After having considered the historical necessity of iconoclasm, we will add however that there is more than one way of looking at the problem. On the one hand it can be argued—as we said at the beginning—that Christian devotion was made simpler and more 'rational' by the evangelical movement, and that modern Western man has benefited from the removal of certain superstitions; on the other hand it can be said that the destruction of art during the sixteenth century represented a loss: a loss in the ability of the Christian mind to generate and sustain a world of symbols which before had made communal life as well as individual life richer from an imaginative and from an emotional point of view. Here is how

---

[6] For the influence Calvin had on Holland, see P. McCrew, *Calvinist Preaching and Iconoclasm in the Netherlands 1544–1569* (Cambridge: Cambridge Univ. Press, 1978).

[7] No systematic work exists in this area; see K.P.F. Moxey, *P. Aertsen, J. Beucklaer and the Rise of Secular Painting in the Context of the Reformation* (New York, Garland, 1977), 109–196; and now also H. Feld, *Der Ikonoklasmus des Westens.*

[8] The most recent surveys of Reformation iconoclastic movements are in Christensen, *Art and the Reformation*, 66ff., and Eire, *The War Against the Idols*, 89ff.; for England see also J. Phillips, *The Reformation of Images. Destruction of Art in England, 1535–1600* (Berkeley: Univ. of California Press, 1973). On the conceptual controversy, see Stirm, *Die Bilderfrage*, on the relationship with Byzantine Iconoclasm, Freedberg, "The Structure of Byzantine and European Iconoclasm."

Carl Jung expressed the ambivalent feelings of modern man, who looks at the destruction of images that took place in Europe in the sixteenth century with mixed feelings of relief and nostalgia:

> The history of Protestantism has been one of chronic iconoclasm. One wall after another fell. And the work of destruction was not too difficult once the authority of the Church had been shattered. We all know how, in large things as in small, in general as well as in particular, piece after piece collapsed, and how the alarming poverty of symbols that is now the condition of our life came about. With that the power of the Church has vanished too—a fortress robbed of its bastions and casemates, a house whose walls have been plucked away, exposed to all the winds of the world and to all dangers.[9]

The psychologist Jung's complaints about iconoclasm are echoed by some historians of religion and art historians. We owe to Mâle the pertinent observation that it was the Reformation that destroyed religious art in the Christian world and that after the Reformation "there will still be Christian artists, but there will not be a Christian art."[10]

\* \* \* \* \*

Images posed problems for some Fathers of the Church and other Church authorities from the earliest times, and especially from the middle of the third century. Precisely at that time, when Christian art first appears in the frescoes of the catacombs, in mosaics, crosses and statues, Church assemblies such as the Council of Elvira (305) and early Fathers such as Tertullian and Origen warn Christians of the danger of images. We even have examples of early iconoclasm: Epiphanius (315–403) tells of how, in a fit of rage, he tore down a veil with an image of Christ he had seen when he entered a church in Anablata. The debate over images took a violent turn during the iconoclastic controversy of the eighth and early ninth century when Byzantine emperors ordered images to be systematically destroyed. While among the many reasons which prompted them to do this there were some important political considerations, the theological

---

[9] C.G. Jung, *Archetypes of the Collected Unconscious*, in *The Collected Works*, vol. 9, pt 1 (Princeton, Princeton Univ. Press, 1969), 13.

[10] E. Mâle, *L'art religieux en France de la fin du moyen âge* (Paris, Colin, 1908), 495.

reasons were certainly significant and sympathetically received, if sometimes criticized and modified, in many parts of the Christian world outside of the empire, as we may judge by the arguments against images which (between 790 and 792) one of Charlemagne's theologians developed in the four treatises known as the *Libri Carolini*.[11]

There was never a period in which images were not questioned. If we turn to a later time, it should be remarked that almost all the so-called heretical movements of the late Middle Ages opposed in various degrees and for different reasons the lavish religious architecture, the sacred images, often the cross itself. A strong anti-iconic position was taken for example by English and Bohemian pre-Reformation movements. Wycliffe was very wary of images, as he believed that "dallying in imagery conceals the poison of idolatry." On this issue his followers were not better inclined than he was, if it is true that "opposition to images can be regarded as one of the most consistent features of the Lollard heresy, and was a criterion for distinguishing its adherents."[12] The same holds true for Huss and many of his followers.[13] It is not surprising therefore that at the beginning of the sixteenth century, when the impulse to reform took such a drastic turn, pervasively shaping a new mode of looking at religion, many theologians decided to tackle the issue in a more systematic way. The first one to do so was Karlstadt.

Andreas Bodenstein was born around 1477 in Karlstadt, from which town he took his name. After receiving his doctorate in theology at Wittenberg in 1510, Karlstadt became interested in the same years as Luther in many of the issues which troubled his more renowned colleague. After 1517 he followed the Reformation, and in the absence of Luther from Wittenberg he moved to radical positions on a number of crucial issues, estranging himself in the long run from mainstream Lutheranism. Bitterly attacked by Luther after 1522, Karlstadt was eventually driven out of Saxony and arrived finally in Switzerland, first in Zurich and then in Basel, where he died in 1541. Among the ideas which characterize his theology and are related to his positions on images are a strong spiritualism, the total refusal of

---

[11] Bevan, *Holy Images*, and Martin, *A History*.

[12] Aston, *Lollard and Reformers*, 136. The quotation from Wycliffe, *ibid.*, 139.

[13] On Huss, H. Bredekamp, *Kunst als Medium sozialer Konflikte* (Frankfurt: Suhrkamp, 1975).

physical aids for spiritual life, the rejection of tradition and intermediation and the assumption of every part of the Old Testament as a binding and ever valid law for the Christian.[14]

Karlstadt addressed the issue of images with enormous, almost fanatical zeal. Influenced, as were other Reformers, by the spiritualism of Erasmus and his rejection of the externals, he stressed from the beginning the absolute primacy of the Word against tradition (in marked contrast to the Catholic polemicists, he virtually never referred to the writings of the Church Fathers or to acts of councils). He also claimed the superiority of spiritual prayer over the observance of the externals, and upheld the validity of the Mosaic commandment against images. Finally, he underlined how the use of images was socially damaging inasmuch as it kept the lower classes away from the Scriptures and delayed—rather than accelerated, as it was supposed to—their spiritual evolution.

Karlstadt's iconoclastic spirit manifested itself already in his works of 1521, when he openly advocated the removal of the images of Christ, the Virgin, and the saints, but it came into full bloom in the winter of 1521–1522. At this time in Wittenberg, in the absence of Luther, several people tried to speed up the pace of change. Gabriel Zwilling, an Augustinian preacher, and Karlstadt took the lead in promoting some important reforms. The reforms advocated by the Wittenberg movement reflect the particular character of the debate at that time, in which the crucial issues were monastic vows, the character of the mass, and the veneration of saints. Since the traditional forms and uses of the mass were subjected to particularly intense criticism and radically changed, it is not surprising that during the movement lateral altars began to be removed and, together with them, their associated images. What is certain is that the activity of the Wittenberg Reformers heated the atmosphere and created a certain unrest, involving some disorderly destruction of images, and it convinced the city council to promulgate, on 24 January 1522, a series of ordinances, one of which required the removal of the images from the churches. It was precisely at this moment that Karlstadt wrote with great enthusiasm his little book *On the Removal*

---

[14] On Karlstadt and the crucial debate between him and Luther on images, see Preus, *Carlstadt's Ordinaciones*; Sider, *Andreas Bodenstein von Karlstadt*; M. Edward, *Luther and the False Brethren* (Stanford: Stanford Univ. Press, 1975); Sider, *Karlstadt's Battle*; and Christensen, *Art and the Reformation*.

*of Images*, dated 27 January 1522, with the obvious intent of clarifying the meaning of the ordinances and of pressuring the authorities to accept the *fait accompli*.[15] Karlstadt thought of the pamphlet as marking the end of a successful process of renovation, but in fact it was the beginning of a long conflict which reached its conclusion in the Protestant world only fifty years later.

There is no doubt that the nature of contemporary devotion lay at the heart of Karlstadt's fierce opposition to images. The cult of images as practised by people in his day appeared to him to be idolatry and polytheism. He never ceases to remind us that worshippers of images offer to them the honour which should go only to God. People embellish them, he says, with gold and precious stones, with silk and damask; what is worse, they place them on altars, bow down before them, and perform all the gestures and rituals of veneration. Karlstadt also correctly relates a variety of other rituals to images. He notes, for example, that pilgrimages often were undertaken by the faithful to implore a special grace from 'miraculous' statues and paintings of particular saints. It is to be said in this regard that Karlstadt does not clearly separate the problem of images from the problem of the cult of the saints. Images, although they have taken a life of their own, are for him above all the medium of the idolatrous cult of the saints. His view, in a way, accords with the traditions of the Church, which held that the use of images helped the faithful to remember and to imitate the virtues of the saints.

Having defined idolatry as the main target of his attack, Karlstadt goes on to define and dismantle the various arguments traditionally used by the theologians of the Church to justify the existence and veneration of images. First, he denounces the doctrine of the prototype, which had originated with St Basil and which stated that the honour given to an image does not rest on that image but passes to what the image represents, that is, its prototype.[16] This doctrine, of course, allowed the defenders of images to deny that the respect shown to images had anything to do with images themselves. Karlstadt argues that by preferring one image to another, or by

---

[15] On the treatise, see Christensen, *Art and the Reformation*, 23ff., and Sider, *A. Bodenstein von Karlstadt*, 167ff. On the Wittenberg movement, Preus, *Carlstadt's Ordinaciones*, and Christensen, *Art and the Reformation*, 35ff.

[16] Basil's theory was reported by John of Damascus in his first oration in defence of images, chapter 21 (tr. Anderson, 29).

believing that the image of a saint has a power independent of the saint, the faithful demonstrate that they attribute to images qualities which transform them into objects endowed with supernatural power and worthy of veneration, into the false or alien gods of the Scriptures.

Another important point of traditional doctrine which Karlstadt attacked was the principle of the so-called relative cult. According to this principle, there are many forms of veneration, not just one, and they may be ranked according to the importance of the object of veneration. Images occupied a relatively low place on a scale that went from *dulia* to *latria*.[17] This was the theory, but in practice the layman was not always able to make a distinction and seemed too prone to revere images, relics, and the Eucharist in an indiscriminate way. Moreover, some people believed, as did Thomas Aquinas, that certain images, such as the image of Christ, did merit the highest form of veneration and that there was nothing wrong in worshipping them. Karlstadt found all such theories disagreeable and certainly incompatible with the belief that all glory should go to God alone. He was inclined to magnify the gap between God and nature, and to remove from the space between them anything—whether human, like the saints, or physical, like images—which tended to attract a cult.

Finally, Karlstadt devoted particular attention to the idea that pictures constitute some kind of a Bible for the illiterate (the so-called *Biblia pauperum*) and that this justified the use of images. The notion was formulated by Gregory the Great in a famous letter of 599 addressed to Bishop Serenus of Marseilles,[18] who had permitted some images in churches to be destroyed, and this formulation, however inadequate it was as a full explanation of the use of images, was regarded as unassailable. In his letter Gregory tells Serenus that paintings and sculptures are the Bible of the illiterate and that only through them can the uneducated masses learn sacred history and dogma.

---

[17] *Dulia* is the reverence accorded the saints, as contrasted *hyperdulia*, the honour accorded the Virgin Mary, and *latria*, the worship reserved for God alone.

[18] Gregory the Great, *Epistolarium*, in Migne, ed., *Patrologia Latina* [hereafter *PL*], vol.77, 1128ff. Gregory also wrote another letter on images to Secundinus in which he elaborated somewhat on the theme, *ibid.*, 990ff.

Karlstadt rejected the idea entirely and asserted that it destroyed the twin foundations of Christian life: the equality of all men before God and the absolute pre-eminence of the Word. "Is it not truly a papist teaching," he writes, "and diabolic distortion that Christ's sheep may use forbidden and deceitful books and examples? Christ says: My sheep listen to my voice. He does not say: They see my image or the images of the saints." In Karlstadt's view, it is because the simple, illiterate people have been confined to a devotion based on meaningless objects that Christians have lapsed into idolatry. Only by turning to the Word can they emancipate themselves.

Such a critique of the Bible of the illiterate allowed Karlstadt to demonstrate that there was a real and evil connection between the power of the clergy—which he opposed—and false doctrine and diabolic practice. The clergy had set itself apart from the laity and assumed a privileged position through its exclusive right to administer the sacraments and by reserving the Scriptures to itself. Karlstadt, by contrast, wanted a single, united Church and vigorously denounced anything that stood in its way, especially images. He saw them "as part of a religious ambience whose function and impact was to retard the intellectual and spiritual growth of the laity, and—more important—to misdirect and corrupt Christian piety at its very center."[19] This attack on the Bible of the illiterate is in complete accord with Karlstadt's insistence that the Eucharist be given in both kinds to the laity. To receive the Eucharist in both kinds would put the laity on equal footing with clergy and this would finally undermine clerical authority.

In his attack on tradition Karlstadt draws almost exclusively upon the Scriptures to provide an arsenal of weapons, the most important and powerful of which are the first and second commandments, to which he refers at least a dozen times ("Thou shalt have no other gods before me / Thou shalt not make unto thee any graven image, or any likeness of any thing that is in heaven above, or the earth beneath, or that is in the water under the earth." Exodus 20:3–4). Before the Reformation these commandments were regarded as rules whose meaning were not necessarily as straightforward and unambiguous as it seems at first reading, but, rather, as laws whose value varies with the time and circumstances. For Karlstadt there is simply

---

[19] Preus, *Carlstadt's Ordinaciones*, 35.

no ambiguity in the Decalogue. Mosaic Law is normative and eternally valid as it stands and prohibition of images, which heads the list of commandments, is the most important and for this reason it is repeatedly emphasized throughout the Old Testament, especially by the prophets.

Much of the best weaponry in the scriptural arsenal used by Karlstadt came from St Paul, whose spiritualism and contempt for the flesh strongly attracted him. Because Paul had said that we do not know Christ after the flesh, Karlstadt concludes that the senses are of no use in understanding the divine and applies to Christian veneration of images the language of Paul's condemnation of idolatry. As a consequence, for Karlstadt the Old and the New Law entirely agree on images, and the views of Moses and Paul on the issue are identical.

*On the Removal of Images* was not composed as a leisurely meditation on a theoretical issue, but was produced in the middle of a heated debate over the actual removal of paintings and statues from the churches of an important German town. This may explain the broken pace of the language, certain excesses (for instance, were some hundred biblical quotes really necessary or desirable in a text of about twenty pages?), and the conspicuous absence of dispassionate reasoning that is underlined by impatient outbursts and interjections.[20] It is not surprising, given the extraordinary circumstances, to find in the text frequent allusions to specific events and issues debated within the Wittenberg movement in 1521, and this is not the least of its interest. This is especially true with regard to the conflict among the Reformers themselves. We know, for instance that the ordinances removing images from the churches of Wittenberg were resisted not only by the conservative clergy but also by some of the Reformers, like Melanchthon, who were concerned that certain reforms might disturb or even alienate those in political power. In the fall of 1521 Melanchthon had expressed the opinion that the Mosaic Law on images was subject to time and no longer applied to Christians, a position not unlike that of the Catholic polemicists, and that St Paul's assertion, "that we know that an idol is nothing in the world, and there is none other God but one" (1 Cor.

---

[20] Whereas *ad hominem* arguments and invective abound, as they do also in the writings of the Catholic polemicists.

8:4), could be interpreted to mean that images were at worst neutral and therefore Christians had some freedom of choice about whether or not to use images. In light of this, Karlstadt's obsessive insistence on the simple literal meaning of the first two commandments highlights a developing theological and political split in the Protestant camp.

Disagreement on how to proceed became an overwhelming obstacle in the relationship between Karlstadt and Luther as soon as Luther returned to Wittenberg on 6 March 1522, hardly a month after the publication of *On The Removal of Images*. Luther annulled the ordinances, suspended the removal of images and mounted a full scale attack on Karlstadt. In the eight sermons of the *Invocavit* of March 1522, as well as in the later treatise *Against the Heavenly Prophets* of 1525, Luther forcefully expressed his point of view on the issue of images: images are 'indifferent,' and Christians have the freedom of using them or not; given the fact that many are 'weak' in the faith or in the knowledge of God, images can actually fulfil a useful function; conversely, destroying images is dangerous because it can be the occasion of scandal and favour political terrorism and extremism (especially in the later treatise, Luther was already concerned with the political disturbances which eventually exploded in the Peasants War). While fighting iconoclasm, Luther became more and more inclined to accept religious art as a relevant component of Christian devotion and his spirituality generated an impressive amount of original art. The controversy also allowed him to refine some concepts of his theology.[21]

The struggle between Luther and Karlstadt developed into a full-fledged debate over a large number of issues, at the heart of which was one crucial for the early Reformation: whether to proceed gradually in matters concerning God's will, or to act quickly and decisively to remove whatever threatened the salvation of the people.[22] At the heart of the debate was also the issue of whether a reformation of devotion should be imposed or brought about by persuasion. While obviously Karlstadt believed in quick action

---

[21] The *Invocavit* sermons are in *Luther's Works*, ed. C. Bergendoff (Philadelphia: Muhlenberg Press, 1958), vol. 51, 67–100; the treatise *Against the Heavenly Prophets, ibid.*, vol. 40, 73–223. On Luther and art, Christensen, *Art and the Reformation*.

[22] Sider, *Carlstadt's Battle*.

directed from above, Luther thought that preaching would be a better way of dealing with erroneous practices, and it is actually believed that the controversy with Karlstadt helped Luther to define his concept, which was to be so relevant in later years, of the freedom of the Christian.[23] In that debate, Luther increasingly gained power, while Karlstadt even lost his right to reside in Saxony. Although he lost in Wittenberg, however, Karlstadt saw his position gain strength elsewhere. As we noted above, the views outlined in his treatise came to be shared by more and more of the Protestant world and entered the mainstream of the Reformation. The intellectual force of Karlstadt's theology found converts and recent scholarship has acknowledged the important influence that his spiritualistic, mystical orientation had on the development of Evangelical Anabaptism, especially in Switzerland and Holland.[24]

Of course, Luther was not alone in challenging Karlstadt. Two of the most important German theologians of the Church took it upon themselves to reply to his treatise: Johannes Eck in an historically based defence of images—*On Not Removing Images of Christ and the Saints*—which clearly states the traditional position of the Church on the use and veneration of images, and Hieronymus Emser in a much longer essay—*That One Should not Remove Images of the Saints from the Churches*—which includes a point by point refutation of Karlstadt's thesis.

Hieronymus Emser was born in Ulm in 1478. He studied theology, law, and classical learning in various universities, and throughout his life he pursued historical and humanistic as well as theological interests. Emser devoted much of his energy, after 1519, to opposing first Luther and then Zwingli on some important issues like the mass, the priesthood, and the primacy of the pope, a task ideally suited to his ebullient temperament. In imitation of Luther he even provided a German translation of the New Testament. He die in Dresden in 1527.[25]

---

[23] See on this point Bernhard Lohse, *Martin Luther* (Munich: Verlag Beck, 1981), 62ff.

[24] Calvin August Pater, *Karlstadt as the Father of the Baptist Movement: the Emergence of Lay Protestantism,* (Toronto: Univ. of Toronto Press, 1984).

[25] On Emser, see *Dictionnaire de spiritualité* IV, 2, and *New Catholic Encyclopedia* V.

Emser published his tract scarcely two months after Karlstadt's *On the Removal of Images*, and dedicated the work on 2 April 1522 to Duke George of Saxony, whose energetic defence of the Catholic faith, he says, was the stimulus to his taking up the pen against Karlstadt.[26] In the preface he discredits the work of his opponent as just one more in a long line of other such clearly heretical attempts to dismantle the Church of God. In the body of the treatise he then goes on to assert that images are, first of all, allowed by natural law, which for Christian theologians was one of three principal sup- ports—together with the Old and New Testaments or Laws—of all moral and religious structures. Images have been for all time, he argues, as much a part of religion as priesthood or any other common devotional practice. They were used by all the people of antiquity, both pagan and Jew. Despite the seemingly clear prohibition of images in Exodus, Moses, at God's command, made cherubim for the tabernacle and also the brazen serpent. The temple of Solomon itself was covered with images. In view of such facts, Karlstadt's interpreta- tion of Mosaic Law is made to appear as a perverse oversimplifica- tion. After all, the prohibitions of Mosaic Law and the writings of St. Paul were not directed against images as such, but against idols and the practice of idolatry. Moreover, he notes that Christians have used images from the time of Christ and that the practice was sanctioned by Christ himself. To support this assertion he relates a number of the legends about early images of Christ; that of Abgar, King of Edessa, to whom Christ sent an image of himself; of Veronica's veil, on which Christ imprinted his features as he struggled towards Golgotha; of the images which St Luke painted of the Virgin and Christ. And he notes, as well, that early historians of the Church, such as Eusebius of Caesarea, reported having seen with their own eyes images of the apostles.[27]

To these precedents, he adds a list of ten reasons supporting the use of images, most of which derive from the three main principles

---

[26] Smolinksy, "Reformation und Bildersturm," 479. Smolinsky's article can be consulted for more information on the treatise.

[27] The reader could usefully compare Emser's treatise with a Catholic pre-Reformation work in defence of images like Pecock's *Repressor*, written around the middle of the fifteenth century; he would discover Emser's total adherence to tradition: R. Pecock, *The Repressor over Much Blaming of the Clergy*, ed. Ch. Babington, 2 vols. (London, 1860), I, 191–207.

justifying images in the medieval tradition (*memoria, Biblia Pauperum, excitatio*). For Emser, images stir the memory and cause people to reflect on the saints; they arouse people to imitate the pious deeds of the saints; they serve as the Bible of the illiterate. Other reasons reflect a new emphasis: images are aids to salvation ("sixthly, so that the beloved saints will be the more inclined to pray for us the more we are seen to be devoted to their service"), to worship ("thirdly, so that the almighty and eternal God together with his saints will be the more venerated by them [the people] if every day they see them before their eyes"), to praise the Lord ("fourthly, so that they [the people] might the more diligently offer thanks daily to God and his saints for the benefit they have received"). Finally, Emser stresses again and again that the veneration of the saints and their images in no way diminishes the glory of God, because the veneration we give saints in their images is clearly distinguished from that which we offer to God.

The Devil and others have always opposed images, of course. Mindful of the old proverb 'out of sight, out of mind,' Jews, Christian heretics, pagans, and Arabs have constantly sought to destroy Christian faith by removing images. Faced by such onslaughts, the Church has repeatedly affirmed the propriety of images and defended their use in several councils (Emser frequently refers, for example, to the acts of the second Council of Nicea);[28] and when it has been necessary, the Church has raised up conspicuous champions for images, such as the Emperor Constantine, Pope Gregory the Great, and Charlemagne.

While the Word was central to Karlstadt's theological system, tradition obviously looms large in Emser's. Every aspect of Catholic devotion is buttressed by reference to tradition and the reader is consequently led through a maze of patristic writings, acts of councils, and legend. There is, as a result, little that is new in Emser's treatment of the theme, apart from the acknowledgement, towards the end of the treatise, that the use of images has been subject to abuse (licentious images of saints and holy virgins, etc.) and should be carefully regulated. To protect the hierarchy, even this acknow-

---

[28] Because it focused particularly on the issue of images. For a recent translation of the decrees of this council on images, see Sahas. Because it focused particularly on the issue of images. For a recent translation of the decrees of this council on images, see Sahas, *Icons and Logos.*

ledgement—a reluctant sop to the Reformer's zeal—is hedged by the claim that such abuses are either the fault of private patrons, who spend too much money for refined and elegant images, or of artists who, for reasons of their own, sometimes produce images more sensual than necessary, and therefore more likely to lead the innocent and weak into temptation, than those of the pagans.

Johannes Maier was born in 1486 in Eck, Bavaria, from which he takes his name. He studied theology in the best German universities of the time and in 1510 he received both a doctorate at Freiburg i.B. and a chair of theology at Ingolstadt. After 1518 he became a formidable opponent of the first generation of Reformers, both German and Swiss, against whom he issued a large number of writings on the most debated doctrinal matters. He opposed both Luther and Karlstadt in 1518 and 1519 in writing and in the Leipzig disputations which remained famous throughout the century.[29] In both his doctrinal work and political positions (he led the Catholic group in opposing the Augsburg Confession in 1530), Eck was one of the most conservative and inflexible polemicists of the century, inspiring with his work a whole generation of Catholic theologians. He died at Ingolstadt in 1543.[30]

Eck's treatise, unlike Emser's, is not a specific response to Karlstadt but a more general defence of the Catholic position on images.[31] Not surprisingly, Eck too gives great weight to tradition, and his arguments in defence of images are very close to those of Emser. It might be noted, however, that the emphasis in Eck's treatise is not so much on a reasoned rebuttal of Karlstadt's arguments as rather on a historical review of the use of images in the history of Christianity, with a focus on the very idea of tradition. Eck opens his treatise with the assertion that the Mosaic prohibition of images no longer has any force because with the Incarnation Christ has become visible; to

---

[29] His *Defensio contra amarulentas D. Andreae Bodenstein Carlostatini invectiones* of 1518 has been edited in this century by J. Greving in *Corpus Catholicorum*, vol. 1 (Münster, 1919).

[30] On Eck, *Dictionnaire de spiritualité* IV, I, and *New Catholic Encyclopedia* V.

[31] It is not clear what exactly Eck knew of the situation, and whether he had read Karlstadt's treatise; he was aware, however, that in Wittenberg *some* Reformers were preparing to remove the images: Iserloh, "Die Verteidigung," 77. See information and bibliography on the treatise, which had various editions, in *Corpus Catholicorum*, vol. 16, ed. J. Metzler (Münster, 1930), lxxxvii.

refuse to represent Christ is tantamount to denying the dogma of the unity in Christ of God and man. It appears therefore that Christ himself, with his coming, has not only justified but has *created* sacred images. Christ has given his followers sacred images the same way has given them the Scriptures.

This is the traditional defence of images based on the Incarnation as it had been expressed by St John of Damascus,[32] probably the single most important medieval defender of images. To this Eck adds a somewhat abbreviated but thorough review of Christian images, reporting (as true) the usual legends of Veronica and St Luke, the story of Abgar, and some passages taken from the Fathers (Augustine, Jerome, Ambrose), the same passages which a long medieval tradition going back to Nicea had always used. It is only at this point that Eck provides the reader with the classic justification of images: images arouse the memory of the saints, stimulate the faithful to emulate them, are the Bible of illiterate (ch. v-viii).

The second half of Eck's treatise is devoted to reviewing the attempts made by the Devil to destroy images through the work of the iconoclasts. In this section Eck gives us a history of Byzantine iconoclasm, derived from the *Chronicle* of Theophanes,[33] dismantling the reasons of the enemies of the Church and pointing at the terrible punishments which God inflicted on them. The sort of arguments that Karlstadt had advance are dealt with in this historical review of the various attacks on images made by heretics and heathens of all kinds, each of which was successfully resisted and overcome by the Church with obvious help from God. The review puts Karlstadt and other Reformers into a perspective that cuts them down to size. In other words, the Reformers' assaults on the faith and their arguments are nothing new, but rather tired retreads of efforts which, like those of past, would inevitably be subdued and pass

---

[32] On the Incarnation removing the Mosaic prohibition see especially the first oration in defence of images. John of Damascus wrote extensively in defence of images, namely one chapter in the fourth book of his *De fide Orthodoxa (De fide Orthodoxa*, bk iv.ch.xvi, in Migne, ed. *Patrologia graeca* [hereafter *PG*], vol.94, 1167ff.) and three long sermons (*Three Orations, ibid.*, 1227–1420). English translations from the three orations were made by Allies and Anderson, for which see the bibliography.

[33] For the Turtledove ed. of Theophanes, see the bibliography.

away. Eck could not image that Karlstadt's treatise was only the beginning of a long war that would actually be won by the enemy.

The treatises of Karlstadt, Emser, and Eck staked out clearly irreconcilable positions on the subject of images that precluded any compromise or hope of resolution. Subsequent contributions to the debate tended merely to restate old arguments and explore new invective.

# Select Bibliography

Aston, M. *Lollards and Reformers. Images and Literacy in Late Medieval Religion.* London: Hambleton Press, 1984.

Baxandall, M. *The Limewood Sculptors of Renaissance Germany.* New Haven: Yale Univ. Press, 1980.

Bevan, E. *Holy Images: An Enquiry into Idolatry and Image-Worship in Ancient Paganism and in Christianity.* London: Hallen, 1940.

Christensen, C.C. *Art and the Reformation in Germany.* Athens, Ohio: Ohio Univ. Press, 1979.

Coulton, G.G. *Art and the Reformation.* Oxford: Blackwell, 1928.

Eire, C.N.M. *The War Against the Idols. The Reformation of Images from Erasmus to Calvin.* New York: Cambridge Univ. Press, 1986.

Feld, H. *Der Ikonoklasmus des Westens.* Studies in the History of Christian Thought, xli. Leiden: Brill, 1990.

Freedberg, D. *The Power of Images: Studies in the History and Theory of Response.* Univ. of Chicago Press, 1989

_____ "The Structure of Byzantine and European Iconoclasm." In *Iconoclasm.* Eds. A. Bryer and J. Jerrin. Birmingham: Birmingham Univ. Press, 1977.

Garside, C. *Zwingli and the Arts.* New Haven: Yale Univ. Press, 1966.

Iserloh, E. "Die Verteidigung der Bilder durch J. Eck zu Beginn der reformischen Bildersturms." *Würzburger Diozesangeschichts-blätter* 35–6 (1974): 75–85.

John of Damascus (St). *On Holy Images.* Engl. tr. M.H. Allies. London, 1898.

_____. *On the Divine Images. Three Apologies Against Those Who Attack the Divine Images.* Engl. tr. of selected passages by D. Anderson. New York: St Vladimir's Seminary Press, 1980.

Jones, W.R. "Lollards and Images: the Defence of Religious Art in Later Medieval England." *Journal of the History of Ideas* 34 (1973): 27–50.

_____. "Art and Christian Piety: Iconoclasm in Medieval Europe." in J. Gutman. *The Image and the Word*. Missoula: Scholars Press for the American Academy of Religion, 1977, pp. 75–105.

Karlstadt, A. *Von Abtuhung der Bylder und das keyn Bedtler unther den Christen seyn sollen*. Repr. and ed. by H. Lietzmann in Kleine Texte für theologische und philologische Vorlesungen und Übungen, no. 74. Bonn, 1911.

Laube, A. *et al* (eds.) *Flugschriften der frühen Reformationsbewegung (1518–24)*. 2 vols. Vaduz and Berlin, 1983.

Martin, E.J. *A History of the Iconoclastic Controversy*. London: Society for the Promotion of Christian Knowledge, 1930.

Preus, J.S. *Carlstadt's Ordinaciones and Luther's Liberty. A Study of the Wittenberg Movement*. Cambridge: Harvard Univ. Press,1974.

Sahas, D.J. *Icon and Logos. Sources in Eighth Century Iconoclasm*. Toronto: Univ. of Toronto Press, 1986.

Scavizzi, G. *Arte e architettura sacra. Cronache e documenti sulla controversia fra riformati e cattolici*. Rome: Casa del Libro, 1982.

_____. *The Controversy on Images from Calvin to Baronius*. Toronto Studies in Religion vol. 14. New York, 1992

Sider, R.J. *Andreas Bodenstein von Karlstadt. The Development of His Thought, 1517–1525*. Leiden: Brill, 1975.

Smolinsky, H. "Reformation und Bildersturm: H. Emsers Schrift gegen Karlstadt über die Bilderverehrung." In *Reformatio ecclesiae*. Ed. R. Bäumer. Paderborn, 1980, pp. 427–440.

Stirm, M. *Die bilderfrage in der Reformation*. Gutersloh: Gutersloher Verlagshaus, 1977.

Theophanes. *Chronicle*. Engl. tr. and ed. by H. Turtledove. Philadelphia: Univ. of Pennsylvania, 1982.

Wandel, L. P. *Voracious Idols and Violent Hands*. Cambridge: Cambridge U. P., 1995.

# On the Removal of Images[1]

by Andreas Karlstadt

## On the Removal of Idols

i. That we have images in churches and houses of God is wrong and contrary to the first commandment. Thou shalt not have other gods.

ii. That to have carved and painted idols set up on the altars is even more injurious and diabolical.

iii. Therefore it is good, necessary, praiseworthy, and pious that we remove them and give Scripture its due and in so doing accept its judgement.

God's houses are buildings in which God alone should be glorified, invoked, and adored. As Christ says: My house is a house of prayer and you make it a murderers' cave [Matth. 21:13]. Deceitful images bring death to those who worship and praise them, as it is written of them: They are strangers to God and completely covered with shame and have become as loathsome as the things they have loved (Hosea 9[:10]). We could never deny that it is out of love that we have placed the so-called saints in churches. If we had not loved them, we would not have set them up where God alone should dwell and rule. Had we been opposed to them, we would have fled them rather than embraced them. Our deeds convict us of loving images. Have we not shown them the honour which we show exclusively to great lords? Why have we caused them to be painted and coloured, to be adorned with velvet, damask, silver, and golden robes? Why do we deck them out with golden crowns? With precious stones? And offer them that

---

[1] The word *bylder* of the sixteenth-century German title is often rendered as 'icons' in English. We have preferred the word 'images' for *bylder* because the modern meaning of the word icon is narrower and calls to mind a specifically Byzantine tradition and the images used in the Orthodox Church. It should also be noted that we have omitted in this translation a long dedication to Count Wolf Schlick.

21

honour and love that we do not willingly give our children, our wives, our parents, our most exalted princes and lords? Who can believe us when we say: We have not loved the idols, the carved and painted images? When our actions have betrayed us? God hates and is jealous of pictures, as I will demonstrate, and considers them an abomination, and proclaims that all men in his eyes are like the things they love. Pictures are loathsome. It follows that we also become loathsome when we love them.[2]

Thus images bring death to those who worship or venerate them.Therefore, our temples might be rightly called murderers' caves, because in them our spirit is stricken and slain. May the Devil reward the popes who thus bring death and destruction upon us. It would be a thousand times better if they [images] were set up in hell or the fiery furnace than in the houses of God.

Now hear more about the nature and origin of the house built for God. Solomon speaks as follows: Thy house, O God, is made solely that there thou mightest regard the devotion of thy servant and accept the prayers that he pours out before thee and thine eyes are upon this house day and night, wherein thy name shall be invoked (2 Chronicles 6[:19–21] and 1 Kings 8[:28–30]). In the same book Solomon enumerates many things which ought to be uniquely dedicated to God.[3] Thus it is especially amazing to me how God has borne and suffered our great evil up to this time.

See! The house of God is made for this purpose, that he alone should rule in it and, as our helper, should open his eyes to us in our need. Further, God alone should be worshipped there. Moreover, only God's name should be invoked there. I would like to know what answer we could give to true Christians and Jews, who have an understanding of the Bible, or even to God, who has given us his teaching through the Holy Spirit, when they or he asks: How is it that you are so audacious as to set up images and idols in my house? How can you be so bold and impudent that in my house you bow down

---

[2] For Karlstadt to insist on the admission 'we have loved images' is in accord with the Erasmian criticism of images, and contrary to the claim of the Catholic theologians that images were seen by people only as signs. The most recent survey of Erasmus' criticism of images—which undoubtedly influenced Karlstadt, is in Eire, *The War Against the Idols*, 28–53.

[3] Karlstadt is referring to 1 Kings 7, which provides a catalogue of materials and objects used in the construction of the Temple.

and kneel before pictures which have been made by the hands of men? Such honours belong to me. You light candles before them. But if you want to set candles burning and blazing, you should do so [only] for me. You bring them wax offerings in the form of your afflicted legs, arms, eyes, head, feet, hands, cows, calves, oxen, tools, house, court, fields, meadows, and the like, just as if the pictures had healed your legs, arms, eyes, heads, etc. or had bestowed upon you fields, meadows, houses, honours and possessions.[4]

Therefore you confess other gods. I heal you and [bear] your [sorrows]. I have nourished them and carried them in my hands and they have not known that I have healed them and borne their sorrows (Hosea 11[:3]). I have redeemed them and they have spoken lies against me. I have taught them and strengthened their arms and they imagine mischief against me (Hosea 7[:13,15]). I have nourished them and raised them up, but they scorn me.

The ox knows his owner and the dull-witted ass the master's crib. But Israel (that is my people) knows me not and my people do not understand the good I have done for them. Alas for the sinful nation (Isaiah 1[:2–4]). I cannot deny, but must confess, that God might in all justice say to our supposed Christians what he said to the Jews. For they run to the idols like crows and ravens after a carcass and fly to a lifeless cadaver. They seek them in particular places, such as Wilsnack in the Brandenburg Mark, Grimmenthal, Rome, and similar places. They bring them tools, silver, gold, wax, and goods as if they were their gods who have delivered them, who have protected them and they are far blinder than the ox[5] in Leipzig or the ass in n.n.[6] who indeed know what good is given them and from whom it comes. So they invoke idols in the house of God and seek health, support, and counsel from insensate dummies. And the people vilify God in his house, which is a good and important enough reason to drag idols

---

[4] The reference is to *ex voto* offerings, often of precious objects, which were left beside images by those who believed that images had conferred some benefit on them.

[5] Not long before writing the *Abtuhung*, Karlstadt had directed a tract against Dr Ochsenfarth in Leipzig. See Lietzmann's edition of the *Abtuhung*, p. 6, n. 18.

[6] The town must have been named in the manuscript. Lietzmann notes a space of about twelve letters in the text where the letters n.n. (*nomen nomen*) now stand, and supposes that the reference may be to Emser. See Lietzmann's edition of the *Abtuhung*, p. 6, n. 19

out of the churches. Not to mention that many a man doffs his cap, which he would wear if his man-made god were not before him. I do not regard it lightly that they bend a knee before the saints. I say more of this in what follows.[7]

That to assume a posture of veneration before pictures is contrary to the first commandment no one should have to learn from me, but, rather, should learn from Scripture. In Exodus 20[:3] it is written: Thou shalt have no other gods. That is to say, you should not attribute the goodness, support, grace, mercy, and forbearance of God to any other but the true God. Learn that through an example: God led the Jews out of Egypt and delivered them from the chains of servitude. They should have attributed that same goodness to no other god. But they made a calf and said: These are the gods of Israel which have led you out of Egypt (Exodus 32[:4]).[8]

That calf was an alien god that had not freed the Jews, and they nevertheless said that it had led them out of Egypt. Thus all men make alien gods when they ascribe the benefits they have received to any but the true God. This is what grieves God himself over and over again in Scripture, as I have said above. That is the reason for which God reproaches Israel: that they chose a king (1 Sam. 8[:4–10]; Hosea 13[:1–2]).

One can make a man into an alien god. A man can proclaim himself to be an alien god, as it is written. Cursed is the man who puts his faith in a man and strengthens his arm. But blessed is the man who puts his hope in God, whose hope is the Lord (Jeremiah 17[:5–7]). That is the reason the Prophets again and again bind themselves with an oath, saying: I will not place my trust in my bow, and my sword will not save me [Psalm 43:7]. You shall not put

---

[7] Karlstadt does not always distinguish between the issue of images and the cult of the saints. The medieval Church had justified images primarily because they helped the faithful to be mindful of the saints and it is natural therefore that Karlstadt, in his zeal to attack anything that stands between man and God, was sometimes not able to separate the two problems.

[8] The verses on idolatry in the decalogue (Ex. 20:4–5) were omitted in medieval catechisms because they were believed to apply *exclusively* to the Jews of the Old Testament. Luther accepted this tradition, as did, of course, the Catholic Church. Karlstadt, like Zwingli and Calvin after him, believed instead that the commandment against images was valid for Jews and Christians alike. On the various interpretations of the commandments in the sixteenth century, see Stirm, *Bilderfrage*, 229ff., and below, note 22.

confidence in princes [Psalm 117:9]. They say this because they will not make any other god and because they want no image in their hearts. They want to confess him alone who cannot be depicted. For God cannot tolerate that.

For this reason God said (immediately after he gave the commandment, Thou shalt have no other gods before me): Thou shalt make no carved or graven image. Thou shalt make no likeness of anything in the heavens above or the earth below or that is in the water. Thou shalt not worship them. Thou shalt not venerate them. I am your God, a strong and vengeful God, a jealous God who punishes the sons for the sins of their fathers (Exodus 20[:4ff.]).

See how God prohibits any kind of image because men are frivolous and are inclined to worship them. For this reason God said: Thou shalt not worship them, thou shalt not honour them. Thereby God prohibits all veneration and smashes the refuge of the papists who at all times do violence to Scripture through their subtlety and make black out of white, evil out of good. Thus if one were to say: Indeed, I do not worship images; I do not venerate them for themselves, but for the sake of saints which they signify. God's answer is short and clear.

Thou shalt not worship them. Thou shalt not venerate them. Make whatever gloss you can, thou shalt absolutely not worship them, thou shalt not bend thy knee before them, thou shalt not light a candle before them. God says: If I had wanted you to venerate me or my saints in pictures, I would not have forbidden you to make pictures and likenesses.

Now I want to prove that Christians must confess that they venerate their idols. The grounds [for the proof]: because they bow and scrape before them (for the sake of dead holy men) I can definitely conclude that they venerate images. For if I venerate a marshal in the name of the prince he serves, I venerate both him and his prince. I venerate the servant as the servant of the prince, and do so before I venerate the prince. Thus it cannot be denied that some of the veneration goes to him as a servant. Therefore, when I venerate an image because of God, I truly venerate that which God has forbidden.[9]

---

[9] The defence of the cult of images rested traditionally on the idea of vicarious veneration (the image taking the place of the saint as the marshal takes the place of the absent prince). According to this theory any cult directed to the image (as respect shown to the marshal) goes to the saint represented therein, so that the

Now I will ask in addition, is it a trifling honour that we call images saints? If we were willing to think clearly, we would find that we deflect honour from the true saints and transfer it to deceitful pictures of them. Therefore, we are calling images saints and attributing sanctity to them.

Moreover, it cannot be denied that it is a great honour to be on the altar. Indeed, the pope deems it such an honour that he permits no pious layman to stand or recline on an altar. It is truly a great and high honour when you put someone in the place where one handles the body of Christ, where God alone should be invoked, on the altar that has been established for the special honour of God, for his own veneration.

Altars were invented so that one might invoke God's name on them, and on them make sacrifices and venerate him alone. For this reason Noah built his altar (Gen. 8[:20]). Likewise Abraham (Gen.12[:8]). Likewise Moses (Exodus17[:15]). Thus God indicated the reasons for altars (Exodus 20[:24ff.]): that his name should be praised and whatever sacrifices one wants to make be offered to him_that one might ever want to make. We offer such veneration to idols when we place them on altars and light candles before them, and when we call upon them in the name of the saints they represent. Everything that we perform on altars we should do for God (Deut. 27[:5?]). Therefore it is never possible to have them on the altars and at the same time wish to deny that we venerate them.[10]

Now because altars were established exclusively for invoking the name of God, it is far more diabolic to put images of the saints on altars than to nail them to walls. This we will discuss in the next section.

Pope Gregory has not forgotten his papist nature and offers to a likeness the veneration which God has given to his Word, and says that pictures are the books of the laity. Is it not truly a papist teaching

---

physical object (like the marshal) is not venerated *per se*. This was the doctrine of the prototype as outlined by St Basil.

[10] In Wittenberg in 1521 the issue of images was intertwined with other controversial issues like the cult of the saints, mass, and sacrifice. Karlstadt speaks of altars because the image of the saints—whether painted or carved—were in fact placed on them. This meant for him that the special symbol of man's worship of God was polluted by idol worship.

and prompting of the Devil to say that Christ's sheep may use forbidden and deceitful books and examples?[11]

Christ says: My sheep listen to my voice [John 10:27]. He does not say: They see my image or images of the saints.

God says: My sheep are the sheep of my pasture [John 10:16]. That is to say, the pasture of my teachings, not the pasture of my images.

Moses says: You shall teach your children the Word of God from their youth. But Gregory says: The laity shall use images for books. Tell me, dear Gregory, or have someone else tell me, what good things could the laity indeed learn from images? Certainly you must say that one learns from them nothing but the life and the suffering of the flesh and that they do not lead further than to the flesh. More they cannot do. For example, from the image of the crucified Christ you learn only about the suffering of Christ in the flesh, how his head hung down, and the like. Now Christ says that his own flesh is of no use but that the spirit is of use and gives life [John 6:64]. Thus Peter too says that Christ had words of eternal life and spirit [John 6:69]. Since, then, images are deaf and dumb, can neither see nor hear, neither learn nor teach, and point to nothing other than pure and simple flesh which is of no use, it follows conclusively that they are of no use. But the Word of God is spiritual and alone is useful to the faithful.

Therefore it is not true that images are the books of the laity. For they may learn nothing of salvation from them, and take absolutely nothing from them which serves salvation or is necessary to a Christian life. I do not want to go on at length and [thereby] give images the veneration which Gregory offers his idols. I note, however, why the popes have put such books [i.e. images] before the laity. They observed that when they pastured their lambs in books [i.e. Scripture] their rubbish market did not flourish. And one would want to know what is godly and ungodly, right and wrong. Paul says that we should persevere in the teaching of Christ [1 Tim. 4:16], and Christ proclaims that he taught his disciples the Word of his Father (John 17[:6]). They never thought of an image.

Christ also says that the truth makes men free and makes them his disciples (John 8[:31–32]). No image can do that. Thus saying that likenesses are the books of the laity is precisely the same as saying

---

[11] The theory of the *Biblia pauperum* was outlined in the writings of John of Damascus, but went back to Gregory I: see Introduction, note 18.

that the laity ought not to be the disciples of Christ, should never be free from the bonds of the Devil, and should also not enter into the godly and Christian life. Paul also teaches that we should have no connection with those who venerate likenesses (1 Cor. 5[:11]), and adds: You should not venerate images. You should flee the honouring of images (1 Cor. 10[:14]). See how Paul hates the reverence of likenesses and how we ought to have nothing in common with those who venerate images thus, even if they do not actually worship them.

Indeed, they say, Paul says that images are nothing (1 Cor. 8[:4]). We also know in our hearts, [they say,] that images are not gods and that there is only one God. Answer: I wish to God that those who use images for books really did know that in their hearts, but I cannot believe it. And did you not also hear that Paul says that we should flee the honouring of images?[12]

Do you not know that Paul says that those who do such things will not possess the kingdom of God [I Cor. 6:9]? How can you bring the laity to the kingdom of God when you offer to a likeness that veneration which God has given to his Word alone? When you put them in the place where God alone should be venerated and invoked? I want now, O Priest, O Monk, to stir your heart and make you come to the conclusion that you cleave to images and have a true idol in the image that the hands of men have made.

Now, finally, you should also take it to heart that I absolutely cannot advise the mortally ill to cling to carved or painted crucifixes.[13] The reason is that they serve no purpose, as has been said, and cannot bring the sick any further than to the physical suffering of Christ, which is of no avail, as Christ himself says: The flesh is of no use (John 6[:64]). It does not please Paul that you know Christ after the flesh. Therefore he says: We do not know Christ according to the flesh [2 Cor. 5:16]. But our image-lovers want the laity to know Christ in the flesh, which avails nothing. They want to teach how Christ hung on the cross rather than why he was hanged. They teach about his body, his beard, his wounds. Of the power of Christ they teach nothing at all. But without the power of Christ no one is saved. So I say, in the first place, that many

---

[12] St Paul's statement that idols are nothing (1 Cor. 8:4) had been used by Melanchthon to oppose a removal of images (N. Müller in *Archiv für Reformationsgeschichte*, 1908–9, 436ff.).

[13] Because the crucifix was believed to have great power over the Devil, one was always kept near someone who was dying. Both Emser and Eck make much of this.

thousands will be saved without the physical presence of Christ, and, second, that images in general are forbidden and prophets have preached against likenesses (Habakkuk 2[:19]). God says: Woe to him who says to the wood, Awake! And to the silent stone says, *Surge* or Rise up! How can a piece of wood or a lump of stone teach? It may well be decorated with silver or gold, but there is no spirit in it (Habakkuk 2[:19]). Behold then how God heaps evil upon those who say to a piece of wood: Wake up! That is, in effect, said when you show devotion to a piece of wood. God also says: Woe to him who says to a stone, Rise up—which is to say—Help me. Thus fools say to the dying when they are caught in the snares of death: See, now you have the Lord Jesus in your hands. Habakkuk says there is no spirit in a likeness. When God rises up, all likenesses fall. Where images sit, God cannot be. As it is written in the fifth chapter of Micah: I will destroy the likenesses in your midst and you shall no longer pray to the works of your own hands [Micah 5:12]. Thirdly, even if I did profess that likenesses should be allowed, which no Christian can, nevertheless there is no consolation except in the Word of God, in which the just man has his life, health, and salvation. Therefore it is incomparably wiser that you recite the two gospel texts which the Lord gave at the end and before his death. That is to say, that you explain to sick and dying man the content and meaning of these comforting words: My body is given for you; my blood is poured out for you for the forgiveness of sins [Luke 22:17ff.]. These gospel texts have a living spirit. The image of Christ is nothing other than wood, stone, silver or gold, and the like. Fourthly, I must tell the Gregorists the story of Bishop Epiphanius who in the time of Jerome removed a cloth from the church because an image of a saint or a crucified Christ was painted on it in violation of the scriptural prohibition. It can be seen clearly from this that early on the Christians hated likenesses and banished them from the houses of God. Epiphanius arrived in Anablatha and there went into a church and saw a dyed and painted curtain on the door which had an image that was a likeness of Christ or of a saint. He says that he did not really know what image it was, but nevertheless he did not want to allow it in the church because it hung there contrary to Scripture. Therefore, he cut down the curtain. This is to be found in the writings of Jerome.[14] Even if I might admit that the laity could learn

---

[14] Migne, ed., *PL* vol. 22, 526. Karlstadt cites Erasmus' edition of Jerome (Basel, 1516. Tomo 3, fol. lxx3. ira. c.). The story is in a letter from Epiphanius to John of Jerusalem which Jerome translated. See Elliger, *Die Stellung der alten Christen zu*

something useful of salvation from images, nevertheless I could not permit that which is contrary to scriptural prohibitions and against God's will. Scripture clearly states that God hates the pictures which the papists call books and is jealous of them. I ask you, if you were opposed in your heart to an image and wanted neither to see it nor hear it, how would you like it if someone wanted to learn about you and venerate you in such a hateful and horrible book [i.e. the book of images]? Without a doubt you would hate and shun me with my little book or image if I wanted to honour you by means of that which you forbid, which you hate, and which you shun. Now God says that he cannot tolerate any image which we make, and that he hates and is jealous of all who love images, as we said above. And Isaiah writes (Isaiah 42[:17]): Those who trust in images shall be tormented with shame.

Note that God made an image of fire. And he ordered a serpent to be made which was not the image of him, but was erected for no other purpose than that those who had been bitten or wounded by snakes might look upon that image and be made whole (Num. 21[:9]). That image was given by God himself and was not created by a human mind. Nevertheless, Scripture praises King Hezekiah (2:18[:4]) for breaking the bronze serpent in pieces because the Jews sacrificed to it.[15]

Our images are not from God; indeed, they are forbidden by God. Still we try to defend them, heedless that the many poor people who offer them candles and money, who kneel and uncover their heads before them, injure and do harm to themselves in that way. Yet we go on defending idols and images, preserve them in the churches, and allow the poor innocent lambs of God to come to grief through such terrible abuse. And we want to honour them as books.

Therefore I must again speak of the uselessness of images. But everything according to Scripture, for I do not desire anyone to believe me or accept my authority. Indeed, may the Devil thank you if you believe me and accept my authority. Turn your ears and eyes to Scripture, which says: The makers of images are nothing and there

---

den Bildern, (Leipzig, 1930), 53–60.

[15] The brazen serpent, the cherubim of the mercy seat and the images of the Temple of Solomon were for the Catholic theologians clear proof that God approved images. Karlstadt, needless to say, mentions the serpent only to record its destruction at the hands of Hezekiah.

is no profit in the most precious and most cherished thing [Isaiah 44:9].

They themselves witness that their images see and understand nothing (Isaiah 44[:9]). Here make note, you idolatrous unbeliever, that the maker of an image is nothing and that his very best work avails nothing. Yes, certainly, they are of no use for salvation. You yourself must confess that you will not ask an image-maker what profits you for salvation because he is a image-maker. How, therefore, can Pope Gregory make so bold as to say, Images are the books of the laity, when artists can teach nothing useful for salvation? Note that your artists can see, hear, and understand and bear witness to the fact that their images can neither see nor hear, nor have understanding. And you do not and ought not to want image-makers as books. How, then, could you take images for books?

How could images be useful to you as books? Who can deny that books are useful? No one. Who may say that images are useful when your maker of images is useless? No one. Now I want to briefly demonstrate that images in themselves are also useless, proving everything with reference to Isaiah 44. He is an evangelical prophet. Isaiah says [44:9–11]: Who has formed or made God and made the graven image that profits nothing? Behold, all the makers and friends of images are shamed. They shall all be gathered together and be frightened and made to tremble.

And he goes on to tell, almost mockingly and sarcastically, how the idols are made and are of no profit [44:12–16].

Nor can I pass over in silence the fact that God cannot suffer any of the bowing and scraping and stooping with which we honour the idols. Thus God speaks through Isaiah.

The maker of images makes an image and bows before it. He bows before it and prays and says: Free me, deliver me, for you are my god [Isaiah 44:17].

Thus, they have forgotten that the eyes of the image do not see and they have no understanding in their hearts and do not consider what they have said before: I have burned half the wood with which I have made this god. And with one half of the branch I have roasted my meat and fired my oven. With the other half I have made this idol. Before this chunk of wood I want to fall down [Isaiah 44:18–19]. At the end of the same chapter God says: I am the Lord who made all things and no one with me (Isaiah 44[:24]).

If I had time and space I would gladly treat Isaiah more thorough-ly, but for the sake of brevity I will begin with the end and then come back to the start, thereby returning to the introductory material. See, and note well, that images in churches are contrary to the first commandment. And that God does not tolerate our placing anything created next to him. Thus he proclaims: I am the Lord who made all things and none with me.

You holy gluttons should mark well that God alone gives aid and no one else with him or beside him. So it must indeed be true (if the truth is to be the truth) that nothing created next to God can help us. Now tell me, you worshipper or venerator of idols, if the saints could not help you, how could deceitful images help you? You want to venerate the saints in images and offer [them] that very veneration which in their lives they shunned and forbade. They, when they were alive, did not allow you to make offerings to them or invoke them, as Peter says: There is only one name among men whereby you may be saved (Acts 4[:12]). If there is only one name, why do you (blockhead) make many names among humankind in which you promise salvation?

Do you not know that they looked at Peter and were amazed and Peter said: You men, what amazes you? And why do you look at us, as though we had made the lame man walk through our own power and force? We have made him whole through faith in the Lord Jesus who the God of Abraham, Isaac, and Jacob sent (Acts 3[:12ff.]). Observe, you fat and rotund image-maker, that in his life Peter forbade you to represent him after his death. Do you imagine that he would now give us another doctrine, and one contrary to that which he gave us when alive? You acknowledge that everything he said and taught [when he was alive] came from the Holy Spirit. Where else would his teaching come from in death? Peter said: You ought not look on us. But you respond to this now by saying: We should not look on images as if they did anything by virtue of their own power.

But listen! If only you spoke the truth. And if only you did not have a personal idol with a greater power over you. But what do you want to say about the revellers' verse: O Saint Christopher, your powers are so great that whoever looks upon you early in the morning shall laugh or live in the evening? Tell me how many thousands of people have paused to gaze for a time upon the image of St Christopher in order that they might be protected from sudden death? And that they might live happily until the night. Have these people not put much hope and trust and sought consolation in looking at depictions of St Christopher?[16]

Because of this scandalous state of affairs you should counsel [everyone] to believe that all images should be dragged down to the Devil. For behold now whether these people do not look up to the image of Christopher as a god.

You must also admit to me that many of the laity take great comfort and put much hope in other images.

Is not this kind of an entreaty called worship? Dear lord come, come, come to my aid. Is that not to say: Dear image free me, save me, preserve me from sudden death?

Look! You have permitted the laity to light candles before images of Sts Paul, Peter, and Barnabas, and bring them offerings, something which the saints themselves, in their lifetimes, shunned like the plague. Nevertheless, if you are the super-clever philosopher, if you are such an erudite fellow, I beg you, in a friendly way, to tell me whether Paul, Peter, and Barnabas would themselves have permitted us to place them [their images] on altars? You must say no and no again. Why do you set their forbidden images on altars, images which they would not have accepted? Note also, my dear friend, that to bow and kneel are forms of veneration which you give to images against the will of God, as was demonstrated in the passage from Isaiah 44 cited above.

Mark also how mad, foolish, and nonsensical are those who give such veneration to images. For Isaiah says [Isaiah 44:17ff.]: They bow before their gods and prostrate themselves and have forgotten and do not understand that their images do not see or hear. They do not understand that they have carved splinters and wood from a log (which they believe to be a saint) with which they have cooked their meat and warmed their rooms. That they do not want to see. Therefore they shall be confounded, shall be afraid and tremble, and shall be destroyed. O how evil it will be for those who, caught in the throes of death, cleave unto idols and bow and kneel before them. It will

---

[16] We alluded in the Introduction to the popular belief that gazing upon an image of St Christopher assured one of not dying in mortal sin during that day. Hence the image of St Christopher was to be found everywhere (Coulton, *Art and the Reformation*, 305). Erasmus, in the *Enchiridion militis Christiani*, cites this as a clear example of how images and superstitions are related. See Erasmus, *Opera Omnia* (Leiden, 1704), col. 26.

be no excuse that they have done this to the saints. God knows their hearts better than they themselves and will accuse them with his Word because they have venerated images. For he said: Thou shalt not venerate them (Exodus 20[:5]).

Now I come back to the beginning and turn to Isaiah, who says: They are of no use (Isaiah 44[:10]).

Books are of use to readers. It follows that images are not books for the laity, contrary to what Gregory and his entire company say.

Listen to what Ezekiel says, you Gregorists and papists! If any man turns away from me and sets his heart upon idols and comes to a prophet and consults me through him, then I will in my own person answer him and will make him a sign and a proverb; I will cut him off from the midst of my people (Ezekiel 14[:7–8]). See here, you praiser of idols, what Ezekiel says about images and do not forget on your life that when you take an idol or image to your heart (as many do, as was said in connection with the image of St Christopher) God will destroy you and damn you and will answer you himself. Thus God answers us in his own words: You shall not look to prophets. But let the man who in these times inquires of doctors, masters, and bachelors of art about such things and does not believe unwaveringly in the voice of the Lord hear what follows in Ezekiel 14 [:9-10]: If a prophet errs, I, the Lord, have made him err and will destroy him from the midst of my people. See how God destroys both the prophet who errs and makes others err, and [also] the man who consults such a prophet. Act accordingly.[17]

If a man knows the prohibition and will of God, he should follow it strictly and listen neither to angels, nor to saints, nor to prophets who want to lure him away from the divine commandment, although they may appear to mean well. The story in 1 Kings 13 teaches this in clear words.

God sent one of his servants to King Jeroboam and ordered him not to eat or drink [in the house of the king]. That prophet or man of God, Semeas,[18] understood God's prohibition, but he allowed himself to be led astray by another prophet, who said: I am a prophet also, as you are, and an angel of God inspired me, saying, Take him back with you in your house that he may eat and drink. Semeas did

---

[17] In all this mention of doctors etc. there may lurk a reference to Luther.

[18] In 1 Kings 13 the prophet eaten by a lion is not named.

that and was disobedient to the Word of God. Therefore God had him torn apart by a lion (1 Kings 13[:1ff., especially verse 24]).

Note that when we have the Word of the Lord and want to be disobedient to the will of God and allow ourselves to be persuaded and deceived by others, we must die. Even if the persuasive but deceitful man takes the form of a prophet, or an angel, or a teacher, or a Christian who performs a good Christian work for you and wants to give you food and drink, if his good deed prevents you from being obedient to the divine words and commandments, you shall not follow him; not even if he were a stout, brawny, fat monk or doctor [of theology]. But if you follow someone because of his position, appearance, beautiful words, and protestations of friendship, and thus fail to observe God's prohibition, you must certainly die (like Semeas) by the lion who walks about in the world seeking whom he may devour [1 Peter 5:8].

Therefore God slew the sons of Aaron, Nadab, and Abihu, because they offered before God an alien fire which he had not commanded (Levi 10[:1ff.]).

Note that when one [of them] ignited a fire which was identical in character and heat to the fire of the Lord, nevertheless, because it was alien, God punished those who offered such a fire.

Accordingly, I say that even though pictures may have the appearance of a good thing, we should nevertheless not tolerate them in churches and among the faithful. For as Balaam had to confess: There is no picture in Jacob and no idol in Israel. This is clearly expressed in Numbers 23[:21] and Exodus 20[:4]. For this reason no Christian or believer should take up images, because he clearly hears [the Lord's commandment]: You shall have no images. The believer shall live according to the Word and disregard appearance, whatever shape or name it might have.

If someone comes and says that images teach and instruct the laity just as books do the learned, then answer him: God has forbidden me to use images and therefore I do not want to learn anything from them.

If someone else comes and says [that] images remind and recall to us the sufferings of the Lord and often bring it about that someone offers an Our Father and turns his mind to God who would otherwise neither pray nor be mindful of God, then you, my Christian, respond: God has forbidden images. Again, Christ said that God is a spirit. All who truly worship God, worship him in the spirit (John 4[:24]). All who worship God in images, worship in untruth. Only in appearance and with outward show do they think on God. But their hearts are foreign to God, and [they] make themselves their own idol in their hearts and are full of lies. As Isaiah in chapter 44[:20] says: Your foolish and silly heart worships them and does not say, I have a lie in my right hand.

Also, no Christian can deny that spiritual prayer is divine work which God alone effects, as it is written in Jeremiah 33[:6]: I shall manifest to them prayer and the worship of peace and truth. What God alone can do, no image can. You also may not say that the image of Christ brings you Christ, for that is not true. No man can come to me except that my Father draw him (John 6[:44]). All who come to Christ must be disciples of God and not be reminded or taught by images to come to Christ.

If you heap together all the images on earth, they still will not be able to offer a single sigh to God on your behalf.

Whenever I want to have an outward admonition and reminder, I should ask for the one which Scripture indicates, not the one which it hates and forbids. I would much rather fall with horse and cart into sore tribulation and distress than come to an image to be reminded of salvation. Isaiah denies that images are of use, yet they would have to be of some use if they were to lead us to God in true thoughts (Isaiah 44[:10]). That affliction outwardly teaches and admonishes and makes us reflect and causes us to know, invoke, and worship God is taught in Scripture: Defeat and vexation give understanding (Isaiah 28[:19]). For you have punished me and I have been instructed (Jeremiah 31[:18]). God chastises us and teaches us, like a father his son (Proverbs 3[:12], Hebrews 12[:6]). God wants us to cry unto him in the day of our trouble (Psalm 85[:7]).

But God does not want us to call on him when we see images. He wants us to hate them and flee from them.

In that day when the Lord is exalted, men will cast away their images and flee from them (Isaiah 2[:17–18], 31[:7]; Micah 5[:12]). From this it follows that images are indeed not books from which we should learn.

A Christian, therefore, can understand that pictures should not be called books. Books instruct. But images can not instruct, as Habakkuk says in chapter 2[:19]. Habakkuk says of a stone idol: Is it possible that it can teach? From that it follows, and there is no gainsaying, that images are not books. For if they were books or could teach what books do, then they would have to teach and instruct. From all this everybody can see that Gregory the pope has indeed taught in a popish, that is to say unchristian, way when he offers pictures to the laity on the pretext they are books.

Scripture compares images and idols to youths and says that in many places the godless commit whoredom with images as whores do with youths. I must be crude and obnoxious, but I am not ashamed to speak as Scripture speaks—straightforwardly. I have shattered their hearts, which have turned from me. I have torn out their eyes which have gone whoring after images (Ezekiel 6[:9]). Again: You have made for yourself images in the shape of men and have been impure with them (Ezekiel 6[:9]). The gold and silver which I have given to you for your ornament you have used to make images and have whored with them. You have taken your clothes and clothed those same images with them (Ezekiel 16[:17–18]). We do that in the case of [Carnival] clowns whom we certainly have no intention of regarding as alien gods, much less being told that they are our gods. However we are open in word and deed before the world to the charge that we take images for gods and give them names and venerate them. For we call the image of the Crucified One a lord god and now and again say that it is the Lord Jesus. We also venerate it as though Christ himself were present. The unholy popes and crazy monks have brought us to this. We also say that this image is St Sebastian and that one is St Nicholas, and the like. Thus we name them as the things God loves, and prove our guilt with our words and deeds that images are our gods; that our pictures are things with which our eyes commit whoredom. And it is true that all who venerate images or seek help from them or worship them are whores and adulterous women (Hosea 2, Ezekiel 16). (At this point I should have liked to settle accounts with a woman, one of the Devil's whores. But I hope she will become open to the guidance of the Holy Spirit. Let this parenthesis be my second warning to her).[19] The Devil's whores who give their gold and silver to images (so that one can make images in churches out of that which God gave them for ornament) are like the whores of whom Ezekiel speaks in the sixteenth chapter as we noted above. They make images and consort

---

[19] The reference is to someone in Wittenberg, not necessarily a woman, who wanted to protect and defend images.

illicitly with them and cover them with their clothes and bring them precious incense, bread, wine, beer, chickens, geese, and horses. And, in addition, they bring them their children and sick friends, regarding which God says: Do you think this childish behaviour is of no consequence and insignificant? We have many writings of this sort which revile the worshippers of images as whores and adulterous women and conclude that churches in which images are placed and venerated ought in all fairness to be regarded as whorehouses.

But all images, whether male, as St Sebald, or female, as Sts Ursula or Otilia or their kind are forbidden and should not be admitted without exception [into the church], as is written in Deuteronomy 4[:16], for Scripture calls such venerators of images whores and adulterous women and such deceitful images men. From this which we learn how highly regarded such idols are in the hearts of those who venerate and worship them.

That is also the reason God said in the first commandment: I am a jealous God (Exodus 20[:5]). He wants to be our only dear friend and that we should ask only him for help and pray to him alone. Thus do Hosea 2 [:24] and other prophets teach (Isaiah 1[:29], 44[:1ff.]).

God knows very well how dangerous and harmful images are and how we can be violated by them in an instant. Therefore, through Moses, he forbade them many times and often caused his prophets to condemn them.

No excuse or pretext can help you, even if you speak a thousand times. You say, I do not venerate the images of saints for their own sake but for the sake of what they represent. Ah, you impious whore, do you think God does not know your heart more profoundly and better than you? If God did not know that someone could so easily make an idol for which he feels nothing, then God would have allowed us to venerate images in names other than his own. Help yourself, cover yourself, and crawl into every hiding place and explain away your deed as you will and can; you will not, after all, slip away from the divine judgement and justice of God which absolutely forbids images and condemns all who carve or praise images or keep and venerate them (Deut. 27[:15]).

Now I want and shall say to all pious Christians that all those who stand in awe before pictures have idols in their hearts. And I want to confess my secret thoughts to the whole world with sighs and admit that I am faint-hearted and know that I ought not to stand in awe of any image and am certain that God expects of his people that they should not stand in awe of images, as it is written: You should not fear other gods, not worship, not venerate, and should not make offerings to them, but only to God (Judges 6[:10], 2 Kings 17[:35]). And I know that God dwelling in me is as small as my fear of idols is great. For God wants to fill our whole heart and will in no way tolerate that I should have a picture before my eyes. And again, when I put my trust in God with my whole heart, I need not ever fear his enemies.

Therefore God or his Spirit in sacred Scripture says: You shall not fear other gods. You shall not pray to them. You shall not venerate them. And he teaches us that it is the same thing to venerate images or to be in awe of them. For this reason I should not fear any image, just as I should not venerate any. But (I lament to God) from my youth onward my heart has been trained and grown up in the veneration and worship of pictures. And a harmful fear has been bred into me from which I would gladly deliver myself and cannot. As a consequence, I stand in fear that I might not be able to burn idols. I would fear that some devil's block of wood [i.e. an idol] would do me injury. Although, on the one hand, I have Scripture and know that images have no power and also have no life, no blood, no spirit, yet, on the other hand, fear holds me and makes me stand in awe of the image of a devil, a shadow, the noise of a small leaf falling, and makes me flee that which I should confront in a manly way. Thus I might say, if one pulls a man's hair, one finds out how firmly it is rooted. Had I not heard the spirit of God cry out against the idols and read his word, I would have thought: I do not love any image; I do not stand in awe before any image. But now I know how I, in this case, stand toward God and images, and how strongly and deeply images are rooted in my heart.

May God confer his grace upon me so that I no longer venerate the Devil's heads (so one commonly calls the images of saints in the church) more than stone and wood. And God grant that I not venerate stone and wood with the appearances and names of saints. Amen. See here Jeremiah 10[:2–5].

From the texts quoted above it follows that Christians should strictly observe God's divine will, counsel, and command, and no longer tolerate images. And this notwithstanding the old evil custom and the pestilential teaching of priests that images are the books of the laity. For God has prohibited the making and keeping of images.

And God grieves deeply and painfully that we seek out images with any degree of confidence. And he says that they make the house of God impure and defile it (Jeremiah 32[:34]).

Thus we have credible and solid proof of our first two articles, namely the testimony of the Holy Spirit.

The proof for the third article flows naturally from the passages of Scripture which have been cited and is grounded on bedrock. Nevertheless, I want to adduce particular testimony for the third article from Scripture.

God says that you shall do it [i.e. remove images from churches]. You shall overturn and overthrow their altars. You shall smash their images. Their groves you shall hack down and their graven images you shall burn (Deut. 7[:5]). We have no divine altars, but rather heathen or human ones, as is pointed out in Exodus 20[:4]. Therefore Christians should remove them in accord with the content of Scripture, irrespective of the fact that they are external things. If you want to venerate God in outward ways or seek him in ceremonies, then you should follow his ceremonies and laws. The secular authorities should remove images and subject them to the judgement to which Scripture has subjected them.

I should also have hoped that the living God, having inspired in us a healthy desire for the removal of images, might have seen the task to its conclusion. But it has not yet happened perhaps because God lets his wrath down upon us drop by drop with the idea of pouring out his entire wrath if we remain blind and stand in awe before things which can do nothing for us.

I know that the authorities will be punished because Scripture does not lie.

Had, however, our rulers accepted divine counsel and fulfilled its command and driven the knavish and seductive blocks of wood from the church under pain of appropriate punishment, we would have to praise them as the Holy Spirit praised Hezekiah, who ripped down images, hacked down groves, and broke up the image which God had given,[20] as is described in 2 Kings 18[:3ff.]. May God will that our lords be like the pious secular kings and lords of the Jews whom the Holy Spirit praises. In sacred Scripture they have always had the power to take action in churches and abolish what offends and

---

[20] The brazen serpent.

hinders the faithful. By divine right they may force and compel priests to expel deceitful and damaging things. Anyone can see this in 2 Kings 23[:4ff.], where it is written that King Josiah ordered the high priest and the other priests to throw out all the vessels, pillars, and the like which were made for Baal; and he burnt them outside the city of Jerusalem. From this everyone should observe how in accord with divine justice priests should be subordinate to kings. For this reason our magistrates should not wait for the priests of Baal to begin to remove their vessels, wooden blocks, and impediments, because they will never begin. The highest secular authority should command it and bring it about. But if they allow images it will be said of them as it was said of Manasseh in a similar case (2 Kings 21[:11ff.]). And if they would say: Our ancestors have established them and we want to follow in their path; Scripture answers: Ammon did wrong, as had his father Manasseh, and followed in the path that his father had taken (2 Kings 21[:20ff.]). As the mother was, so is the daughter. Your mother is a Hittite and your father an Amorite (Ezekiel 16[:45]). God cannot endure that we help ourselves through subterfuge, by saying, As our elders have gone, so will we go.[21]

Certain image-kissers say: The Old Law forbids images; the New does not. And we follow the New, not the Old Law.

Dear brothers, may God protect you from this heretical statement and prevent you from ever saying it. We do not follow the Old Law, and we do not accept it because it belongs to people who are not Christians and violates and trivializes the teachings of Christ. For Christ based his teachings on Moses and the prophets. And he says that he did not come to destroy the Law but to fulfil it (Matthew 5[:17]). And he also instructed his disciples how he had to live and suffer so that the Scriptures would be fulfilled. Christ also did not violate in even the slightest way the Law of Moses. He also added nothing nor took anything away from the Law of Moses. In short, Christ destroyed nothing which pleased God in the Old Law. Christ upheld the letter and spirit of the Old Law. Whoever can join together these two maxims, to wit, We preserve the Law through faith, and

---

[21] Karlstadt advocates an orderly removal of images regulated by the secular authorities, which, in fact, was being done in Wittenberg under the ordinances issued by the city council (see Preus, *Carlstadt's Ordinaciones*). That reformation of the Church should be in the care of secular authorities was a principle shared by Luther, but rejected, of course by the Catholics.

Through faith or grace we establish the Law, understands Moses, the prophets, Christ and Paul. As for the claim that the Old Law is not binding, it is too much for me to deal with here, especially since I know the enemies of the Law would not understand me. Therefore I want to reply as follows to the opponent mentioned above: My dear friend, you say that the Old Law forbids images. For that reason you will give them a place in the houses of God and pay little attention to that commandment. Why do you not also say that we are not obligated to honour father and mother because that is forbidden in the Old Law? Moreover, murder, adultery, theft, and similar crimes are forbidden in the same tablets in which images are forbidden. And the commandment forbidding images stands at the head of the list as the principal and greatest one. The commandments forbidding adultery and theft, etc. come after as the lesser and least.[22]

Why do you not also say: We want to permit adultery, theft, murder, and so on in churches because those crimes are forbidden in the Old Law?

Christ shows the Law to him who asks: What should I do that I may have eternal life? Why should I not, in this case, also direct you to the Law of Moses? You say that Isaiah and Jeremiah are evangelical prophets and they forbid images. Why does it annoy you that they forbid images? I say to you that God has forbidden images to no lesser degree and no less expressly than murder, theft, plundering, adultery, and the like.

Finally, you must acknowledge that Paul is a great preacher of the evangelical and New Law. He penetrated the depths of the Mosaic Law and brought it to light. He announced the Christian promise, offering consolation beyond measure. You must also say as follows: if Paul forbids images, I must flee from them. Now listen. Paul says: They have exchanged the splendour of the immortal God not only for the likeness of mortal man but also for images of birds, beasts, and creeping things (Romans 1[:23]). Do you hear how evil and damaging Paul thinks images are? He says that those who praise images steal the splendour of God and offer likenesses of creatures. Therefore they diminish God and scorn him. Therefore, Moses again

---

[22] As mentioned above, Karlstadt believed the commandment prohibiting images was valid for all time. This was part of his approach to the Old Testament at large, which he saw as generally binding on Christians.

and again says that God cannot tolerate our images and likenesses. Thus Paul and Moses agree. I have also demonstrated from the Epistles of Paul, cited above, that no one comes to God when he venerates images.

# That One Should Not Remove Images of the Saints from the Churches Nor Dishonour Them and That They are Not Forbidden in Scripture

by Hieronymus Emser

To the most serene, high-born Prince and Lord, Sir George, Duke of Saxony, Landgrave of Thuringia and Margrave of Meissen, my gracious Lord, I Hieronymus Emser, Your Princely Grace's humble and obedient chaplain, offer my fervent prayer and all blessings from God. Gracious Prince and Lord, since Your Princely Grace recently issued a decree in which you, as a loyal good shepherd offered to commit life and property to your subjects and flock in matters of faith, it is my duty, as the least of that same flock, to listen to the voice of my shepherd and to follow him in any way possible. [I] have therefore dedicated this my response to Karlstadt's heretical book about the removal of our beloved holy images to Your Princely Grace in everlasting memory and testimony of your praiseworthy Christian disposition, so that those who come after us and read the above-mentioned heretical book may not only find defence against and response to it, but may also learn from this preceding letter that although this and other heresies have sprung up in the land of Saxony in our times, it has truly grieved Your Princely Grace, being, by the grace of God a most praiseworthy prince and duke of Saxony, and [that you] therefore have, for the glory of God, spared neither life nor property to suppress that heresy, at least in your territories. I humbly request that Your Princely Grace deign to accept this from me in gracious judgement and keep me, as hitherto, in gracious protection. Issued at Dresden, Wednesday after the fourth Sunday in Lent [2 April] in the Year of the Lord 1522.

**Preface**

The recent bridegroom Andreas Karlstadt of Wittenberg has once again composed a Beghardic little book on the removal of images, not invented in his own head, but, rather, cadged from books by Wycliffe and Huss.[1] He has smeared a little honey on this poisonous thing (since it is a bit bitter), namely [what he says] regarding the protection of widows and orphans and [the assertion] that no one should beg anymore.[2] In addition, he says that prelates, abbots, and abbesses should free their brothers and sisters from their vows and deliver them out of their religious orders back again into the world—that is, send them from the dry land back into the deep sea, from paradise back into hell. This time I will let those three additional honey-sweet little tidbits stay in their syrup. However, he lays this charge against images: that they have ears but cannot hear, eyes but cannot see, hands but cannot grasp. And he does this because he assumes there is such a thing as a living image that might look at him in a friendly way and grasp and embrace him. If by some miracle (of the kind one often hears about) one of our carved or painted images could speak, it would undoubtedly answer Karlstadt and say: Our ears were not placed on our heads so that we could hear. We were not given eyes so that we could see, nor hands that we might grasp, but only to indicate the way beyond and call to people's minds those whose shape and figure we represent.

But you, Karlstadt, have ears which were made to hear, still you will not hear your Mother, the Christian church, against whose law and contrary to your own solemn vow you have taken a wife—not into an honourable marriage, which as Chrysostom instructed Diodore the Monk, can never more be, but into an illegitimate union, to the vexation of your brothers and to the eternal damnation of your poor soul. Moreover, you have eyes you can open and close, yet still

---

[1] It is not clear why Emser singles out the Beghards as primary enemies of images, but he is certainly correct in connecting Karlstadt with the tradition of Wycliffe and Huss. On Wycliffe and images, see M. Aston, *Lollards and Reformers* (London, 1984); on the Hussite movement and images, H. Bredekamp, *Kunst als Medium sozialer Konflikte* (Frankfurt, 1976). The phrase 'recent bridegroom' calls attention to Karlstadt's marriage in January of 1522.

[2] Emser refers here to a second, briefer part of the treatise, *Und das keyn Betdler unther den Christen seyn sollen* (And there should be no beggars among Christians), which has not been translated in this volume.

you are blind with seeing eyes. You have hands which are moveable, nevertheless you cannot grasp the thick cloud and darkness of your grievous error. And though the almighty God has given you and your companions the great grace to know him, you have not glorified him nor been thankful to him, but have been obstinate in your thoughts and benighted in your foolish hearts, for professing yourselves wise, you have become fools (Romans 1[:22]).

Such and similar answers might Karlstadt meet if images could speak. Inasmuch as they were not made, nor placed in churches and upon altars so that they could speak, I, Hieronymus Emser, an unworthy priest, feel called upon to open my mouth on their behalf to defend the honour of God and our beloved saints and to exonerate the whole Christian church together with the most holy Pope Gregory (whom Karlstadt arrogantly and falsely accuses of having written or taught in an unchristian way regarding images)[3] from a specious accusation and respond with sound arguments [in its defence]. Therefore, at the very beginning, I call upon the merciful and living God for grace. And I ask the most holy Virgin Mary and Pope Gregory, whom I just mentioned, together with the whole heavenly host and all pious Christian hearts, to pray for me so that I may write the simple truth and prevail over this Beghardian Doctor and force him to make a public response.

Because Karlstadt prefaces his little book with three heretical propositions, I would like here to oppose them with three others which are Christian and which read as follows:  1. That we have images in the churches and houses of God is just and in accord with the commandment, Thou shalt not worship other gods. 2. That to have carved and painted images on altars is both useful and Christian. 3. Therefore it is heretical and unchristian to remove them because Scripture (and the way we use them) gives no grounds to condemn or forbid them.

To establish these conclusions, I will divide my book into two parts. First, I will tell when and why the Christian church accepted images and also what opposition it has suffered for a thousand years on their account. In the second part I will repeat all Karlstadt's arguments, unravel them, and make it apparent that he has [either]

---

[3] See Karlstadt, note 11.

not understood the passages of the Bible which he introduces into his discussion, or has wilfully perverted and falsified them.

## About Images in General

Just as the whole world is divided into three sects, namely Jewish, pagan, and Christian, so images are divided into three groups, namely Jewish, pagan, and Christian. With respect to materials there is little or even no distinction among them, since they are all made of clay, gypsum, wood, brass, lead, gold, silver or other metals. Or they are painted on canvas, paper or panels. But in their significance, use, sense, and meaning there are quite noticeable differences. For as St Augustine teaches in book 20 of *Contra Faustum*, chapter 22, there are many other things which Christians have in common with Jews and pagans and there is no other distinction except in faith, customs, and meaning. Thus there have been priests among Jews and pagans, just as among us Christians. There is, however, obviously a big distinction between the priesthood of Christ and the priesthood of other peoples.[4]

Now I have written about our Christian priesthood against the arch-heretic Martin Luther to the point that he has been compelled to make a public response to me. I would like to try the same thing with Karlstadt, who has an even thicker head than Luther, and see whether I might bring him back to the right path and give him good instruction especially regarding the three propositions on images made above.

## On the Origin, Use, and Meaning of Jewish Images in Particular

Enos, son of Seth and grandson of Adam, made the first image among the Jews, as various Hebrew books indicate and St Jerome sets forth in his *Book of Hebrew Questions*.[5] So also Scripture, Genesis 5 [actually 4:26], says of him that he was the first to call upon the name of the Lord.

---

[4] Emser is saying that images, like priesthoods, are *natural* and that what makes Christian images different from pagan is that the latter are images of false gods (that made them *idols*). He restates this position several times in the treatise, but this, of course, is the point on which Karlstadt would never have agreed.

[5] Jerome, *Librum Hebraicarum questionum in Genesim*, in Migne, ed., *PL*, vol. 23, 994.

The use of this image and the intention of Enos was good, for although the Jews attributed idolatrous worship to him, as though he had carved an idol for himself contrary to the commandment in Exodus 20, nevertheless, our Christian teachers excuse him for this because, first, the Law of Moses had not been handed down at that time, and, second, because he invoked the name of the Lord and not the image. And he made the image for himself solely as a reminder that he might think more often on the Lord. This is what Peter Comestor has to say on Genesis 5: Perhaps he formed the image to stimulate the lazy-minded, just as is done now in the Church.[6] Hugh of St Victor, following other writers, also recalls the story. Not only the Bible, but also the noble Jew, Josephus, in Book 1 of *The Antiquities*, bear witness that Enos, like his father Seth, was pleasing to God and a pious man. He says that Seth, who was indeed an exceptionally pious man, had left children behind him who were also pious and led holy lives and dwelled on the earth peacefully and without any dispute until the end of their lives. Thus Josephus.[7] This Enos was also, on the plane of nature, a figure of Christianity and of all who will thus be praised in the future eternal life, as St Augustine explains in Book 15, chapters 18 and 21 of his *City of God*.

Further, we find yet more images among the Jews which God himself ordered them to make, as (Exodus 25) he commanded Moses to cast the two cherubim in gold and place them on the high altar. Again, there was the brazen serpent, Numbers 21. The Temple of Solomon was also full of paintings and images for which God himself had provided the specifications, as we may read in many chapters of Kings and Chronicles. And that is not without a hidden meaning, as in aftertimes our Christian teachers, inspired by the Holy Spirit, have explained and revealed. From all of this it seems clear that to make and use images in an appropriate way is opposed neither to Scripture nor God. For if every image was forbidden or an abomination before God and defilement of the churches (as Karlstadt, in his silly head, will force Scripture to say), then God himself would not have given the commands mentioned above to Moses and Solomon nor caused the temple and the tabernacle to be thus stained.

---

[6] Petrus Comestor, *Historia scholastica,* in Migne, ed., *PL*, vol. 198, 1080.

[7] Josephus, *Antiquities* 1, 68–72, in *Josephus*, Loeb Classical Library, 8 vols. (London, 1930 ), vol. 4, 33.

Nor do the anxious efforts of Paulus Ricius to twist this command-ment of Moses and claim that it is an exception to the general law hold any water.[8] For if that commandment (You shall not make a carved image, etc.) is not a separate one, but a comment or exposi-tion of the first (You shall have no other gods), as he himself confesses and the Venerable Bede testifies in chapter 19 of his book on the Temple of Solomon, why would it have been necessary to except the cherubim who were never included in that first command-ment? For indeed Moses ordered them to be made not as gods, but as angels of God with wings attached to each shoulder. But this, for the present, suffices regarding images among the Jews.

## Of the Origin and Misuse of Images among the Pagans and Their Idolatry

The first pagan image, from which all idol worship descends, Ninus, the king of Assyria, caused to be made in honour and commemora-tion of his father, Belus. He set this image up in the market place in the middle of the city of Babylon and gave freedom and security for life to all who sought asylum by it and called upon it, even if they had committed murder. For this reason the image was greatly revered and given divine honour and Belus, or his image (according to Berosus in Book 5 of his *Antiquities*)[9], was named Jupiter Babylo-nicus because he founded the city of Babylon, the construction of which was completed by his son Ninus and the queen Semiramis.[10]

The Devil arranged for the misuse of this and other pagan images in order to elicit divine veneration for himself. To accomplish this he spoke to the people first through the image of Belus and afterwards through others, made them ill and then caused them to recover, and taught them how to worship and make sacrifices to him. Thereby he so blinded and deceived them, that they considered the images not just images but rather living gods. And they put such trust and faith

---

[8] Paulus Ricius, *De Mosaicae legis mandatis.* Published in Johannes Pistorius, *Ars cabalistica* (Basel, 1587); modern, unchanged reprint (Frankfurt, 1970), 223ff.

[9] An indirect reference to the *Babyloniaka* of c. 293 B.C. , of which fragments survive in various sources, including Josephus. See P. Schnabel, *Berossos und die Babylonisch-Hellenistische Literatur* (Leipzig, 1923).

[10] That pagan idolatry began with the veneration of a statue erected by Ninus to his father Belus (Baal) was an euhemeristic tradition accepted by Thomas Aquinas in his discussion of idolatry, *Summa*, II, II, Q. 94, art. 1–4.

in them that they slew and sacrificed their own children to them. Indeed, in Carthage alone the people, in order again to propitiate their idol Saturn, once slew two hundred noble children and sacrificed them to him. The authority for this is Lactantius, *Divine Institutes*, Book l, chapter 21.[11]

These pagan images and idols through which the Devil is invoked and God is robbed of his divine honour, are an abomination before God and have been condemned not only by canonical Scripture but also by the wise and intelligent pagans themselves. As Trismegistus says to Asclepius in his book on the power and wisdom of God: See, Asclepius, how even you doubt that this is the case. You do not believe that statues are living and conscious, filled with life and do many mighty works and predict future events.[12] So also (as Lactantius writes, and also Tertullian in the Apology) Socrates was executed in prison in Athens by being forced to drink the cold hemlock—which in Latin is *cicuta*—because he said that there could not be more than one true God. Pythagoras, Plato, Aristotle, and other enlightened philosophers also shared this opinion. Whoever wants to know more about the origin, use, and and false beliefs regarding the oft discussed pagan images and idols must read Lactantius, Augustine, Varro, and Cicero, all of whom have written much on the subject, for I have undertaken to write about our Christian images and not about those pagan idols.

**On the Origin, Use, and Law of Christian Images in Particular**
The ancient, trustworthy, and saintly teacher John of Damascus[13] records the history of the first image of Christ our Saviour in Book 4, chapter 16 of his book *On Orthodox Faith*.[14] King Abgar (who first,

---

[11] Lactantius, *Divinarum Institutionem*, in Migne, ed., *PL,* vol. 6, 233.

[12] Hermes Trismegestus, *Aesclepius,* 2, 24a. The text which Emser supplies varies somewhat from the text in Walter Scott, *Hermetica* (Oxford, 1924), 338, and the translation has been modified accordingly.

[13] From the time of the Byzantine controversy to the sixteenth century, John of Damascus' orations in defence of images were the most important source of inspiration for those who defended images. A recent English translation of this work is, St John of Damascus, *On Divine Images*, trans. D. Anderson, (New York, 1980).

[14] John of Damascus, *De orthodoxa fide*, in Migne, ed., *PG,* vol. 94, col. 1174. John mentions the story only in passing. It is more fully related in Eusebius, *The*

as Eusebius also testifies in Book 1, chapter 5 of his history of the Church) wrote a letter to the Lord asking him to come to him and offered him the half of his kingdom. Because the Lord did not want to come to him, Abgar sent a painter who was to make a portrait of him. Since, however, the blessed face of Christ shone so brilliantly that the painter could not see, the Lord himself impressed the image of his face on a cloth and sent it to the king, by whom it was received with joy and held in great reverence (as was appropriate). There is also an old and believable story which has come down to us that the Lord Jesus impressed the image of his face and figure on the veil of the holy woman Veronica and left it behind him at the end of his life. Afterwards she brought the veil with the image to the emperor Tiberius in Rome, and the emperor (who was cured of a terrible sickness by it) issued an edict saying that Christ should be worshipped as a god by one and all. This edict was annulled by the Roman Senate because it was issued without their knowledge, as Suetonius also reports in his life of Tiberius. And this was done according to divine plan since Christ wanted to be proclaimed and revealed by his disciples and not by a secular power.

In addition, the great Athanasius tells, in his book on the passion of the image of Jesus,[15] of an image of Christ which Nicodemus, the secret disciple of Christ, painted with his own hands and after his death left to Gamaliel, the teacher of St Paul. Gamaliel left it to James the Less, James left it to Simeon, and Simeon left it to Zaccheus, who kept it until the time Titus and Vespasian dared to besiege the city of Jerusalem. At that time, those among the people who believed in Christ were warned by the Holy Spirit to flee Jerusalem and betake

---

Ecclesiastical History, trans. K. Lake, Loeb Classical Library (London, 1975), vol. 1, 89ff. The various legends concerning early and miraculous images, so frequently cited by Catholic polemicists like Emser (the story of Abgar, the image made by Nicodemus, the portrait of Christ and Virgin painted by St Luke, etc.) are thoroughly examined, together with their textual sources, in Ernst von Dobschutz's classic study, *Christusbilder: Untersuchungen zur Christlichen Legende* (Leipzig, 1899).

[15] *De passione imaginis,* in Migne, ed., *PG,* vol. 128, 89ff., is published among the *Spuria* and is certainly not by Athanasius. Dobschutz, *Christusbilder [Beilagen],* 280, noted that the story of the image of Christ by Nicodemus enjoyed particular favour with the polemicists because the pseudo-Athanasian text was accepted by the second Council of Nicea, whereas the story of St Luke's portraits, by contrast, was merely a matter of old, respectable tradition—*constans fama.*

themselves to King Agrippa in Syria (where they would be safe) because Agrippa was a good friend of the Romans. Thus the image, among other things, found its way to Beirut, which lies between Tyre and Sidon[16] and there was hung on a wall in a house. Later that house together with the picture (which had been forgotten, perhaps by the will of God) was bought by a Jew. Finally, the said image fell into the hands of Jews, who spit upon it, drove nails into it, and subjected it to all those indignities which earlier Christ had suffered at the hands of their fathers. At the last, one of them took a spear and drove it through the side of the image, from which blood and water flowed so freely that it was possible to fill a large barrel. They took that to their synagogue and anointed their sick, lame, and blind, who were all healed. Because of this miracle they looked into their hearts and felt guilt and suffered on account of their sins. They then went to the bishop of the city, who took them into his favour and they were all baptized. There was also such a great rush of people to the blood that the bishop had to call a council at Cæsarea in Cappadocia to deliberate concerning it, as one reads in the little book mentioned above, which, among other books by Athanasius, has been recently printed.

Further, John of Damascus writes that he had heard an old story that the holy evangelist Luke had painted [portraits of] Christ and his excellent Mother Mary with his own hands and that these pictures were afterwards brought to Rome. (John writes as follows in the book mentioned above: We have heard that the apostle and evangelist Luke painted the Lord and his Mother, and the images are in the renowned city of the Romans.)

Eusebius, who was referred to above, in Book 7 [chapter 18] of his history of the Church, mentions an image of Christ which the woman who had an issue of blood for twelve years and who was healed by touching Christ's garment set up in the city of Cæsarea, where she was citizen, as a memorial of her eternal gratitude. Eusebius, who was a bishop in Cæsarea about three hundred years after the birth of Christ, saw this image with his own eyes and he bears witness to the great miracles that it performed. Afterwards Julian the Apostate, an enemy of Christ, had the image thrown down and his own set up in

---

[16] Emser has his geography wrong. Beirut lies to the north of both Tyre and Sidon.

its stead. Then a bolt of lightning smashed that statue to pieces. And the citizens of the city set up the image of Christ in its previous place, as Cassiodorus says and we read in Book 6 of his *Historia tripartita*.[17]

Because of such miracles the Christian emperors Theodosius and Valentinian caused a special act to be incorporated into imperial law forbidding anyone to draw, incise or engrave an image of Christ on the ground or other unseemly place and decreed severe penalties as punishment for such a crime.[18]

Both in the East and West there are many well-known stories. For example, during the great plague which occurred in Rome in his time, the holy Pope Gregory organized a 'station' or procession to Santa Maria Maggiore. And he had the image of Mary (which St Luke, as we have said, painted) carried before the people on a standard. Angels of God appeared hovering in the air beside the image, did reverence to it, and began to sing the joyful song *Regina cœli* which St Gregory concluded with the *Ora pro nobis Deum*. And as further testimony there is another story of how one of the same angels appeared above the Fortress of Trajan with a bloody sword in his hand which he then returned to its scabbard as a sign of peace. Afterwards and from that time forth the fortress was called the Fortress of the Holy Angel as an eternal memorial of this event.[19]

Bishop Eusebius writes in Book 7 of his history of the Church that he saw images of the apostles Peter and Paul that had been painted long before his day and were in his lifetime still much copied and held in great veneration.

These are the first Christian pictures of which I have read. Now if Karlstadt and his crowd have more faith in pagan writers of lies than in our own Christian teachers, and in the recklessness of their unstable minds consider the above stories apocryphal or wish to deny them altogether because they are not in the Gospels or other canonical Scripture, I answer with the holy evangelist John who says in his last chapter [John 21:25] that not all the miracles which Christ performed are contained in the Gospels. Just as there are also many

---

[17] *Historia ecclesiastica, dicta tripartita*, in Migne, ed., *PL*, vol. 49, 1057.

[18] The Theodosian Code did indeed forbid the representation of crosses on the floors of churches: Codex Justinianus I, VIII. See *Codex Justinianus*, ed. P. Kruger [Berlin, 1929], 2, 61.

[19] The Castel Sant'Angelo, which incorporates the mausoleum of Hadrian, not a fortress of Trajan.

things which the holy apostles arranged and decreed that are not to be found in their Epistles. Paul commanded that these regulations and laws were to be observed just as if they had been set down in black and white, saying in 2 Thess. 2[:15]: Therefore, dear brethren, stand fast and hold the regulations and laws you have been taught, whether by our letter or our word. Whoever then scorns such or other Christian rules and refuses to maintain them, Paul places under the ban in the following chapter, 2 Thess. 3 [:6], saying: We declare to you, brothers, in the name of our dear Lord Jesus Christ, to withdraw and hold aloof from every brother who does not follow the rule and law you have received from us. Therefore, no man should scorn Christian law, for all the succeeding popes, bishops, prelates and, above all, the Christian councils have for all time the self same power and authority to decree and establish what is appropriate, useful, and pious for Christendom that Peter and Paul and the others enjoyed. This is a view I have frequently and steadfastly defended in my previous books.[20]

I find a number of reasons why the revered early Fathers clung to the use of images in the church and set them up for veneration. The first of them that I cite is drawn from Paul's first Epistle to the Romans (Rom.1[:19–20]), namely, that we must come to an understanding of the invisible through these visible things. For, as Aristotle also teaches, one cannot learn anything except through the five external senses. Thus whatever we want to learn, understand or know must come to our minds through seeing, hearing, smelling, tasting or touching. Therefore, because not everyone can read, write or always hear a sermon, or because what someone has already heard is easily forgotten, images are put before the eyes of simple, unlearned folk so that by means of the information contained in the images they might consider the sufferings of Christ and what kind of life this or that saint led or through what virtues he earned a place in heaven.

Second, so that through such observation they will be stimulated to virtue and devotion and to follow in the footsteps of the saints.

---

[20] Emser applies to images the principle that the tradition and the authority of the Church have a relevance equal to that of Scripture, a principle defended vigorously by the sixteenth-century Church in answer to the *sola scriptura* of the Reformers.

Third, so that the almighty and eternal God together with his saints will be the more venerated by them if every day they see them before their eyes.

Fourth, so that they might the more diligently offer thanks daily to God and his saints for the benefit they have received.

Fifth, so that they will the more willingly serve God and his beloved saints when they can see the rich reward which God gives his elect.

Sixth, so that the beloved saints will be the more inclined to pray for us the more we are seen to be devoted to their service.

Seventh, so that through the intervention of the saints we may also in the end come to this reward.

Eighth, that there may be a distinction between churches and other kinds of buildings. For if there was no image in the church, one would not know whether it was a church or a dance hall.

Ninth, because Christians do not take their revered images for living things or for gods, but only for types and signs of God and his beloved saints.

Tenth, because if one may put up the figure and image of someone on his grave or elsewhere as a memorial to that person's virtue and charity, why should we not permit the images of our beloved saints to stand before us as reminders of their blessed lives?

For these and other reasons our beloved early Fathers made it the rule to have images in the churches and on altars and to venerate them. And therefore they held that since it was not a sin for the Jews to look upon the two cherubim and other images in the Temple of Solomon, so it should be counted even much less as a sin for Christians to look upon a crucifix and images of the beloved saints.[21]

Now, although images of the kind described above were introduced in the times of the apostles and afterwards by the early Fathers were left to us in churches and on altars to glorify God and his saints and to stimulate us to daily reflection and improvement of our lives, nevertheless the Devil (since the veneration accorded him through images in earlier times was withdrawn through the prudence of the early Fathers and redirected to God and his saints) has spared no

---

[21] The historical evidence suggests the contrary. Many early Fathers were opposed to images, which nevertheless had become almost universally accepted by the fifth century; see W. Lowrie, *Art in the Early Church* (New York, 1969), 9ff.

effort to eradicate such images and has used all manner of people for that purpose, namely, Christians, Jews, pagans, Turks, tyrants, and certain heretics. They have all undertaken to throw down our images so that the veneration of God and his saints might be the more easily extinguished, since what is out of sight is out of mind. However, they have never, thank God, been able to do it and also never shall be able to until the Antichrist himself shall come, so help us God.

First, since images are not specifically permitted and are also not specifically forbidden in canonical Scripture, certain bishops of old—such as Epiphanius, Serenus, and others[22]—depending on the letter alone and guided by wilful[23] rather than correct opinion, not only did not want to tolerate images in their churches but where they found them caused them to be destroyed. I will have more to say about this in the second part of this book. And that was the first attack against images by our own people, that is to say, by Christians.

Second, the Jews first attached themselves to Mohammed, the Lawgiver to the Turks, and attempted to destroy Christian images. For not only the renegade monk Sergius but also seven rabbis of the Jews were always with Mohammed and they helped him write the Koran, as Richard reports in his refutation of the said Koran.

Furthermore, Sigebert in his *Chronicle* of the year of our Lord seven hundred and twenty-four tells how a Jew deceitfully persuaded a Saracen king by the name of Gizid that if he removed images from his entire kingdom he would live for forty more years. The king did this and immediately afterwards died a miserable death. And in our own times Paulus Ricius in his commentary on the Mosaic Law mentioned above suggested that because of the affection which the stubborn people had so long had for images, the early Fathers did not wish at the beginning to eradicate them all at once by force, but rather allowed the people some use of them, just as circumcision and other ceremonies were allowed for a time to the Jews. But now that Christians have been confirmed in their faith one should dispense entirely with images, just as with circumcision. Ricius' suggestion (made after he was baptized and became a Christian) may have

---

[22] On Epiphanius and Serenus, see Karlstadt, notes 11 and 14.

[23] Emser's text reads *milder,* but this cannot be what he means. We have supposed it is a misprint for *wilder.*

been offered in good faith, but it is in no way to be accepted by the churches. There is, after all, a big distinction between the circumcision, which, as Paul writes to the Galatians [Gal.5:11], is no longer of use, and images which serve and lead us daily and call God and his saints to mind, as we have shown above. Moreover, if the early Fathers smashed and overthrew the idols and images solely by means of the holy cross of Christ, as we read in their legends, and did so in the temples and in front of the pagan idol-worshippers, how much more easily might they have also removed or smashed our images if they had regarded them as damaging? And this is the second attack against our images as made by Jews, Turks, and Saracens.

Third, certain tyrannical emperors, such as Julian, Philippicus, Leo II (or III according to Platina[24]), and his son Constantine IV (for others V)—all misled by the Devil and certain renegade monks—persecuted and set fire to our beloved holy images and undertook to uproot them utterly with such intense determination that the emperor Leo even banished his own brother who was a patriarch in Constantinople. His son Constantine summoned a *conciliabulum* in Constantinople and forced the bishops to swear to him on the cross to remove all images from all their churches. They absolved themselves from this oath at the second Council of Nicea, as we read in the Canon of Session 22, q.4. In the time of Constantine as well, he not only confiscated the possessions of those laity who refused to comply but also took many lives. Priests were exiled or slain, as all the chroniclers record, and especially Ivo of Chartres, Sigebert, and Cassiodorus in his *Historia tripartita.* And under no emperor was more Christian blood spilled than under this Constantine the Iconoclast.

Fourth, the much mentioned images have also suffered attacks from heretics and first of all from Arius, Faustus, Vigilantius, and others whom Athanasius, Cyril, Augustine, Ambrose, and other early Fathers opposed. Then afterwards, about a hundred years ago, images were attacked by Huss and Wycliffe, and now, in our times by the dregs and scum of all heretics, Andreas Karlstadt of Bodenstein, in this unchristian little book of his. For all these reasons,

---

[24] Bartolomeo Platina, Italian humanist, Vatican Librarian under Sixtus IV, and author of *Lives of the Popes (Liber de vita Christi ac de vitis summorum pontificum omnium,* Venice, 1479).

the holy popes and the entire Christian church were long ago moved to assemble to settle this difficult issue, the subject of so much debate, and through the grace of the Holy Spirit to consider what to do or permit in regard to it.

Thus Pope Constantine I was the first to call a council in Rome and with support of approximately a hundred bishops, proclaimed the emperor Philippicus to be a manifest heretic and made it known that images inspire us, Christian people, to virtue and to imitate the holy saints, to further the service of God and for these reasons should remain in the churches. Therefore, the Romans would not accept the image of Philippicus on coins, letters or seals. Thus also they did not pray for him in the churches.

Similarly, the succeeding popes Gregory III and Stephan III also called councils to deal with this matter, according to Platina. Gregory excommunicated Leo and Stephan excommunicated Constantine. They declared them both to be heretics and proclaimed that the decrees of the Conciliabulum of Constantinople, which Constantine had called against the will and without the knowledge of the pope, were invalid and not binding. The Romans at that time would have immediately elected another emperor had the pope not restrained them with his eloquence and urged them to be patient.

Because, however, Constantine would not retreat from his tyrannical ways, his persecution of images and other heresies, on account of which all of Constantinople was hostile to him, Pope Hadrian and the patriarch of Constantinople by the name of Tharasium called a general council in the city of Nicea (called the Seventh Ecumenical Synod). There four hundred and fifty worthy bishops and other prelates were assembled. They excommunicated all those who break images (whom they call in the Greek language *eikonoklastes*) and declared them to be heretics. They also composed an article setting out the way we Christians may and ought to venerate images, which reads as follows:

### DECLARATION OF THE COUNCIL OF NICEA
### REGARDING THE VENERATION OF THE IMAGES OF SAINTS

Christians do not believe that the venerable images of their beloved saints are gods, nor serve them as gods, or expect salvation or consolation from them, but only in meditation and reflection venerate and worship those whom the images represent. They offer divine veneration or service neither to images nor any created thing.

Since, however, Constantine and his successors, even after this Council had been held (in which the empress Irene herself participated), did not refrain from the persecution of images and from other heresies, Pope Hadrian, and after him, Leo III finally—after prolonged pleading by the people of Rome—took the Empire from the Greeks by lawful judgement and in the place of God and the apostles St Peter and St Paul bestowed it upon the Germans in the person of Charlemagne. Charlemagne, as Lupoldus writes, immediately summoned all the bishops from France and the German lands to a council in Frankfurt-am-Main, to which the pope also sent two worthy legates. They unanimously condemned as a heretic Bishop Felix, who had advised that images should be removed from the churches, and renewed the decree and decision of the Council of Nicea that one should venerate the images in churches and on altars.

Thus, through the piety of the German emperors, and their fear of God, images were left in peace for almost six hundred years until Wycliffe in England and Huss in Bohemia stirred up the old, extinguished flame and with the prompting of the Devil created such a stir that once again the pope and the emperor had to call a council in Constance to deal with the matter. There Wycliffe was condemned by all Christian nations and Huss and his companions were burned to ashes. And once again all those who would now or ever presume to destroy images were declared to be heretics.

Therefore, my friend Karlstadt should not be angry if I call him a heretic inasmuch as he was judged a heretic before he was born not by one, but by six or seven councils. And I marvel much regarding this poor man that he has not considered these things before he subjected himself to such opprobrium and peril. For it is no more possible for him to overthrow so many Christian councils than it is for a fly to drink up the sea. Here, then, I have concluded the first part of my little tract on the origin, use, understanding, and rules governing Christian pictures and how they have been regarded from the beginning up until our times.[25]

---

[25] The history of iconoclasm provided here by Emser is the traditional one presented by Byzantine sources. The first Protestant rebuttal was that of H. Bullinger, *De Origine erroris* (Zurich, 1528, and later editions); Eire, *The War Against the Idols*, 86ff. On the acts of the second Council of Nicea referring to images, see now D.J. Sahas, *Icon and Logos: Sources in Eighth Century Iconoclasm* (Toronto, 1986). On the history of Byzantine iconclasm, E.J. Martin, *A History of*

**The Second Part of the Tract**

In this second part of my tract I give assurance at the outset that it is not my intention to deal with every useless utterance, but to respond only to the most significant arguments which Karlstadt has introduced into the debate. For who could or would rehearse or repeat so much silly prattle without burdening or annoying the readers? In the second place, imperial law has also forbidden under pain of severe punishment any one, whether cleric or secular, to contest or dispute further anything which has once been unanimously decided by a council.[26] The law states: No cleric or soldier or anyone of whatever condition of Christian faith shall publicly address a crowd so as to cause a disturbance or a loss of faith. For if someone disputes those things which have once been duly and justly resolved, he violates the judgement of the most holy synod. And further: Therefore, if a cleric has attempted to debate publicly on religion he shall be removed from the company of clerics. But if a soldier should do so, let him be discharged from service.[27] For this reason I do not intend to reopen this question of images or call into doubt the many councils which have dealt with it but want only to demonstrate the truth to the common, unlearned people for their most needful instruction, and to dispose of the false argument Karlstadt brought forth against the spirit and meaning of Scripture.

Having set down these conditions, I will not take a long time to marshal my forces on this field of battle or practice fencing before a mirror, but, rather, will immediately challenge the man and ride out against him.

KARLSTADT

God's houses are buildings wherein God alone should be venerated, invoked, and adored. As Christ says: My house is a house of prayer, etc.

EMSER

The Divine Majesty alone should be venerated and worshipped inside and outside the houses of God in the highest degree, which

---

the Iconoclastic Controversy (New York, 1930).

[26] Emser frequently cites civil and canon law. We have relegated the citations in the form he gives them to the notes. Here *Codice de summa trinitate et fide catholica, lege Nemo.*

[27] *Codex Justinianus,* ed. P. Kruger [Berlin, 1929], II, 6.

in Latin is called *cultus latriae,* that is to say, as a god and creator of all things to whom we and all things in his power are subjected. Esther 13[:9–10] O Lord and omnipotent King, all things are placed under thy power and there is none who can resist thy will: Thou hast made heaven and earth...etc. Also, he alone has the power to give us or take from us all good things. Every good gift, every perfect gift, comes from above, from the Father of lights (James 1[:17]). Next, one may venerate and invoke the most holy Virgin Mary both in and outside the churches in the highest measure, which in Latin is called *cultus hyperduliae,* because she is the highest and most worthy of all created beings and therefore the angel says she is full of grace and all the Christian churches call her the Mother of God, a Queen of Heaven, and our Lady of the world. Third, we may and should invoke and venerate the revered saints; not as gods, but as followers of God; not as creators but as ones who were created; not as ones who give or take away, but as patrons and intercessors. This, in Latin, is called *cultus duliae.* In precisely the same way in this worldly realm (which is a figure of the heavenly realm) His Imperial Majesty is venerated in the highest measure because he is the lord of the secular and Christian government[28] and all things are under his sway.[29] After him we show deference and bow before all the others who are of high rank, such as kings and princes, just as Paul (Romans 13[:1]) and Peter (Peter 1) have bidden us to do. And this is not only not something not opposed to the emperor, but accords with his command and solemn wish. Therefore, he also punishes severely those who deny princes this honour or presume to scorn them.[30] Third, we also respect all other men in whom we perceive honour, virtue, ability or nobility, as the holy apostle has also taught us: Give pride of place to one another in esteem (Romans 12[:10]), and, Honour all men (1 Peter 2[:17]). And just as such things do not injure imperial dignity, so also the Divine Majesty is not in the least disturbed that next to him we venerate and call upon the saints in an appropriate way. On the contrary, whosoever scorns the saints also scorns God and will in time be punished, just as the fire of hell ignited the throne of the emperor Valentinian because he did not stand up before St Martin

---

[28] *lege deprecatio ff ad legem Rhodiam de iactu.*
[29] *8 di. quo iure.*
[30] *Codice ad legem Juliam Maiestatis 1. Quisquis.*

and did not deign to show him any respect. For this reason Christ did not say: My house is a house wherein one should venerate or call upon me alone, but, rather: My house is a house of prayer.

Karlstadt wants to fortify his opinion with the words of Solomon, who said to God: Lord, this is your house in which your name alone shall be invoked (2 Chronicles 6; 1 Kings 8). [But these words] should be understood to refer to the veneration of the Supreme Creator, as I shall explain below, where Karlstadt says that God alone gives assistance and the saints can never help us.[31]

### KARLSTADT

Deceitful images bring death to those who worship and praise them, as it is written: They are strangers to God and completely covered with shame and have become as loathsome as the things which they have loved (Hosea 9[:10]).

### EMSER

If one has never trusted someone, then that person cannot deceive him. Now we Christians seek no solace in images or place any trust in them. Therefore, they are not able to deceive us. But Karlstadt not only says that images are deceitful, he also calls them scoundrels and murderers and says that they bring death to those who worship them. The written word also does that to its reader as St Paul says in 2 Corinthians 3[:6] *littera occidit* / the letter kills or murders. But that only applies to those who are not willing to govern their souls and beliefs according to the understanding, teaching, and usage of the Christian church, but, on the contrary, pursue their own opinions. But whoever learns first from the Christian church how Scripture and images should be understood will certainly not be slain.

Karlstadt has cited falsely the words of Hosea, since the prophet is not talking about our images, but, rather, about pagan idols and their worshippers. The text is as follows: But they went to Baalpeor and separated themselves unto that shame; and their abominations were according as they loved. Do you hear, Karlstadt, that the prophet is speaking about the idol Baalpeor? How then can you be

---

[31] Emser is here outlining the traditional Church view on intermediation and on the various degrees of honour (ranging from *dulia* to *latria*) which go to the different objects according to their different merit. This doctrine is known as the doctrine of the *relative cult*. The position of Karlstadt is that honour should only go to God.

so presumptuous as to force his words to apply to our beloved holy images? But just as you once had a schoolmaster, so you have also learned how to interpret Scripture.[32]

KARLSTADT

We can indeed not deny that it is out of love we have placed the so-called saints in churches. Had we not loved them, we would never have put them there.

EMSER

It is not a failing that we Christians have set up images out of love and not enmity. We love them not for their own sakes, but rather for the sake of those to whom their features refer and call to our minds. Therefore, we love the saints far more than images of them. Karlstadt, however, has not yet demonstrated that such love is a sin, just as he has also not proved that one ought not to offer them the honour as stand-ins for God or the saints, by removing one's hat or cap or by kneeling before them, which we often offer to a mere mortal. Or that we should not adorn them with velvet, silver, gold or precious stones of the sort which one often drapes over an evil woman.

With respect to his saying, Let the Devil reward the popes who thus slay and bring death to us, it has been sufficiently demonstrated above that it is neither pope nor image, but rather we ourselves who slay and bring death to ourselves when we scorn the Christian church and her teaching in this or other cases. I will say nothing here of how Karlstadt and the other heretics might more justly be called murderers than the images, inasmuch as their writings kill more people than all the images in the world. Karlstadt will not have time to grow a grey beard before we, in the presence of God, answer that we place holy images in his house and venerate them in appropriate ways because if God can tolerate them [the saints] in heaven, he can undoubtedly permit them in the churches, especially since he himself said: Where I am, there also should my servants be (John 12[:26]). I would very much like to know what Karlstadt would say if one of the saints, and especially St Gregory, said to him: How can you be such an envious fellow that you begrudge us the veneration which God and all the world does not? Or how can you be such a coarse

---

[32] A reference, presumably, to Wycliffe or Huss, from whom, at the beginning of the treatise, Emser claims Karlstadt has taken all his ideas.

brute that you deal with the popes in such a dishonourable way and believe yourself to be more wise than all Christian teachers?

### KARLSTADT

You light candles before them. You bring them wax offerings in the shape of your afflicted leg, arm, eyes, etc. Thus you confess other gods.

### EMSER

We do not in this way confess an alien god, for whether we go to Rome or to Aachen we nevertheless pray to the same God we pray to at home. In whatever place God hears us, we acknowledge him and give thanks to him for his grace. But that we must attribute the grace received from God more to the intercession of the saints than to our own efforts and therefore should venerate and honour them is sufficiently argued by Jerome against Vigilantius, by Augustine against Faustus, and by Ambrose against the Arian heretics, as I have written at somewhat greater length concerning this matter in my first book directed against Luther's Reformation thesis on pilgrimages, to which I refer the reader. Therefore all the Scripture which Karlstadt cites regarding idol-worshippers, and especially about how the Jews worshipped a calf and attributed God's help and beneficence to it, as they also worshipped the head of an ass in the desert, according to Cornelius Tacitus and Tertullian, has nothing to do with us Christians since we, as I have said above, do not worship the saints or their images as gods.

Karlstadt cites three authorities, namely 1 Samuel 8 [:4–10], Hosea 13 [:2], and Jeremiah 17[:5–7], to testify that a man could make for himself an idol if he puts hope in himself or in another. For Scripture says: You should not trust in princes [Psalm 117:9] and, Cursed is he who places his hope in a man and strengthens his arm [Jeremiah 17:5]. To this I answer that although our hope (inasmuch as it concerns salvation) should in the end be centred on God alone, nevertheless God has established kings and princes, and we trust in them to rule over us in a way consistent with salvation and to do everything for the best. So we may not be damned nor accused of idolatry for doing that which Scripture has ordered us to do. For indeed St Paul says that every soul should be subject to higher powers (Rom. 13[:1]). But he who wants to have a great deal to do with princes for his own profit or some other business, and not for the sake of God, thinks only that if he acts correctly and as one worthy of a legacy and also adapts in the right way to the business at hand, then there is no difficulty. But if he should find himself on a dun horse,[33] then he may not complain to me if not everything is obtained for which he hoped and made his clever schemes.

### KARLSTADT

For this reason God said (immediately after he gave the commandment: Thou shalt have no other gods before me), Thou shalt make no likeness of anything in the heavens above or the earth below or that is in the water. Thou shalt not worship them. Thou shalt not venerate them. I am your God, etc.

### EMSER

All this, as I have also mentioned in the first part of this work, is nothing more than an elaboration and explanation of the first commandment, namely that we should not worship alien gods. It is not forbidden to us to paint or carve images and to venerate and worship them, except those we worship as idols. That is the meaning of the last phrase, namely, I am your God. It is though he wanted to say: The images which you believe to be gods are not gods. Thus the Venerable Bede says in his book on the Temple of Solomon, chapter 19: There are some who think that by the commandment in Exodus 20, where Scripture says: Thou shalt make no carved or graven image, Thou shalt make no likeness of anything in the heavens above or the earth below, etc., all images were forbidden. They would not say this if they reflected on the brazen serpent, the two cherubim and other images which God himself commanded to be made. Therefore, if we look carefully at the words of Scripture, we discover that, contrary to what they say, it was never forbidden us to carve, make, worship or venerate images except in the way the misguided pagans do, namely as living gods. Thus the Venerable Bede.[34] It follows from this that is not papists, as Karlstadt falsely claims, but he and other heretics who seek hiding places, do violence to Scripture, make black white and good evil.

### KARLSTADT

Now I want to prove that Christians must confess that they venerate their idols. From the fact that they bow and scrape before them (in the name of dead holy men) I can definitely conclude that

---

[33] Stroking a dun horse was proverbial for sycophant flattery. The sense here is that if one engages in such flattery, one should not be surprised if it fails.

[34] *Liber de templo Salomonis*, in Migne, ed., *PL,* vol. 91, 791.

they show veneration to the images. For if I venerate a marshal in the name of the prince he serves, I venerate both him and his prince.

EMSER

This proof is lame in both legs. For such veneration is not offered to a marshal *pro subiecto*, as a Hans or Peter or whatever his name might be, but *pro forma*, because he is the marshal. Otherwise he would perhaps not be venerated in such a way. So also we show reverence to images not for the sake of the material of which they are made—whether stone, wood, gold or silver—but because of the form and shape of those to whom they refer. The wood, stone or other materials remain unvenerated. For all the honour one gives the image (as the great St Basil says) is transferred and attributed to the exemplar which the image represents. Thus John of Damascus in the chapter *On Images* in Book 4 of *On Orthodox Faith* says that frequently when we are otherwise not mindful of our Lord, it happens that we see a crucifix before us, fall down and worship, not the wood or material, but him whom it depicts and represents, just as we do not worship the paper or material on which the holy Gospels are written. For what would the cross be (if Christ were not on it) other than another piece of wood?

Thus, also, we worship the image of the holy Virgin Mary not for the sake of the material from which it is made but because of what is represented. For all the honour which we show to her is transmitted to him who was born of her. Thus John of Damascus. Karlstadt's conclusion that when I venerate an image for the sake of God or one of his saints I honour it in the true sense, which God has forbidden, is false and misleading. For God has not forbidden us to venerate all images, but only the images of idols, as Bede showed above and as has been clarified several times by the Christian councils cited above.[35]

KARLSTADT

Now I will ask further, is it a trifling honour that we call images saints?

EMSER

The poor forgetful theologian Karlstadt does not remember or perhaps has not read that St Augustine excused this simple speech of the people who call images saints but do not really believe them

---

[35] On the doctrine of the prototype, see Karlstadt, note 8.

to be saints (Book 2 *ad Simplicianum,* towards the end),[36] saying as follows: Thus in common speech we are accustomed to give images the names of those whom they represent, for how could we call a painted image of a man anything other than a man? In the same way, when we look at a history painting we say: That is Hector, that is Achilles, here is Rome, here is Troy, etc., although there is nothing there in fact but painted images and figures. Thus although cherubim are celestial spirits and powers, we nevertheless call the images of them which Moses and Solomon had cast in metal cherubim. Hence Scripture says (1 Kings 7) King David went in and sat down before the Lord, but this does not mean the Lord was there in the flesh. It means, rather, that David had sat down before the ark of the Lord. Thus St Augustine. Therefore it does no harm that we call images saints as long as we do not believe them to be saints. And I do not believe there is a Christian man so crude or stupid as to believe images are saints and worship them. And even if one should find such a simple person, the good mother Christian church takes these and similar errors of the simple, which cannot do great damage, into her maternal lap, just as she does with those who, when they hear that God created heaven and earth, think that he made it with his own hands just like a craftsman makes an instrument. As Augustine has neatly explained in Book 12, Chapter 27 of the *Confessions*: For some when as they read, or hear these words, presently conceive that God like some man, or like some unlimited power endued with huge bulk, by some new and sudden resolution, did outside itself, as it were at some distance, create heaven and earth, [even two great bodies, above and below; wherein all things were to be contained. And when they hear God say: Let that thing be made, and it was made; they think the words to have had beginning and ending, to have sounded in time, and so to have passed away; immediately whereupon, the thing became in being, which was commanded so to do: and such other like conceits, which their familiarity with flesh and blood causes them to imagine.] In whom, being yet little ones and carnal, whilst their weakness is carried along in this humble manner of speech, (as it were in the bosom of a mother) their faith is wholesomely built up etc.[37] Thus Augustine.

---

[36] *De diversis quaestionibus ad Simplicianum,* in Migne, ed., *PL,* vol. 40, 143.

[37] The text of the quotation is taken from *St Augustine's Confessions,* trans.

KARLSTADT

Furthermore, no one can deny that it is a great honour to stand on altars.

EMSER

We Christians do not deny that we place images of saints on altars to venerate them and not defame them. But Karlstadt has never proved that offering such veneration is a sin or against God. For as was said above, if God can bear to have the saints with him in heaven, he can without doubt easily tolerate their images next to his image, which is of much lesser moment. What Karlstadt says about how altars were made so that God alone might be invoked and sacrificed to on them, just as Noah, Jacob, Moses and the others built altars to God alone, cannot be turned against us Christians, since whatever we do, sacrifice, celebrate mass or otherwise perform on the altar is done solely in eternal praise of and gratitude to God. So if one says that this is the altar of St Anne and that the altar of St Lawrence, it does not mean that they are truly established for those very saints, but rather that they are dedicated in their memory and in their names to the almighty God, who is not jealous of his own but of others, like the Devil whom he cannot tolerate on altars or have anywhere near him.

KARLSTADT

Pope Gregory has not forgotten his papist nature and offers the veneration to a likeness which God has given to his Word, and says that pictures are the books of the laity.

EMSER

I cannot understand of what Karlstadt is accusing St Gregory, when indeed Basil, Athanasius, Eusebius, John of Damascus, and Augustine, all of whom lived long before St Gregory was born, have written, and it is a common maxim among the learned, that Scripture is speaking pictures, but pictures are silent Scripture, which pictures are also called *zoographia* or living Scripture by the Greeks. According to the words of the Holy Father John of Damascus, no one can really imagine or picture God in his divine essence. Nevertheless God appeared to us on earth not, as he did to Abraham, merely in the

William Watts, Loeb Classical Library (London, 1958 ), vol. 2, 355. Emser quotes St Augustine in Latin but omits several lines. They have been restored here in brackets.

form of a man, but as an actual man in substance and nature (as he even worked miracles and suffered), who was crucified, died, was buried, and arose again. All of these things are recalled and taught to us in Scripture. But since not every one can read or write, or is too lazy to read, the Fathers have permitted such things to be presented to them through painted or carved images, and that they be guided to reflection not only by the image of Christ, but also [by images] of his worthy Mother Mary and those of the other saints. Thus John of Damascus in the chapter of *On Images* mentioned above. Therefore St Gregory stands vindicated.

Then Karlstadt mockingly asks and says, 'Tell me, dear Gregory, what good are the laity able to learn from pictures? Therefore, I ask Karlstadt in return, what good indeed have he and his friends learned from books? Or what more can the letter do than be a sign which signifies and indicates something, which images also do? It follows from this that not only the images but also books show us only the sufferings of Christ in the flesh, and that neither image nor letter, but only the spirit, as Paul says, gives life. Second, it follows that Gregory has done nothing contrary to Moses, Christ or Paul, for it is one and the same thing that Moses, Christ, and Paul have directed the learned to books while Gregory has directed the illiterate to images. It is of no moment whether we learn the Word and will of God from books or from images—similar kinds of evidence produce identical judgements. Therefore Karlstadt has here unfairly and presumptuously chastised St Gregory and he may well have some concern that in time he will be punished, for an old proverb says that it is not good to revile the saints.

Karlstadt falsely cites three passages from Paul against our images—1 Cor. 5; chapter 10 of the same epistle; and Gal. 5, for in these three passages St Paul spoke of serving idols, not of images, as the text makes perfectly clear.

### KARLSTADT

I want now, O Priest, O Monk, to stir your heart and make you come to the conclusion that you cleave to images and have a true idol in the image that the hands of men have made.

### EMSER

If you cannot reason more consequentially than you have hitherto, then all your blood-stirring [battle-cries] can cause no wounds. I want, however, O Karlstadt, to convince you with a few words and to prove that you yourself are an idol and a worshipper of idols.

Whenever a heretic creates a new opinion and believes it to be better than the teaching of the Christian church, he makes an idol to himself in his heart. He then paints or carves it when lets his opinion see the light of day in writing. And finally, he worships it when he regards it as if it were the Gospel. In Baruch 1[:22] we read: We went our way, each following the promptings of his own wicked heart, serving other gods, which the Christian teachers interpret literally as referring to heretics. All the things which are revealed in Scripture regarding the Jews who denied Christ can be said of the heretics who abandon Christ. The author of this is Jerome on Hosea.[38]

### KARLSTADT
Now finally you should also take it to heart that I absolutely cannot advise the mortally ill to cling to carved or painted crucifixes. The reason is that they serve no purpose, as has been said, and cannot bring the sick any further than to the physical suffering of Christ.

### EMSER
This foolish and heretical advice, contrary to the custom of all Christendom, Karlstadt supposes to be based on the words of Christ in John 6[:63], that the flesh is of no use. St Augustine, in the book *Christian Instruction*, answers this and says that the flesh alone and without the spirit is of no use. Nevertheless, it is important to the extent that in gazing on things of the flesh the soul awakes and is enraptured in a spiritual observation of the bitter sufferings of Jesus Christ. Since, then, much rests on this matter—not just for the sick, but also for the healthy—I shall not be loathe to set down when the reader will not be loathe to hear what St Augustine has advised in this matter and how he consoled a mortally ill brother in Book 2, chapter 2 of *On Visiting the Ill*, saying, among other things: Most dearly beloved brother, before all things hold fast to the faith without which no one can please God. In the first place there are those things such as the most worthy sacraments, the holy Trinity, and other matters in which we believe in God alone and over which we must not argue or dispute much since they are matters too elevated for us. Next, there are those things concerning his only begotten Son, our dear Lord Jesus, which are more closely related to us, more common and more understandable. Thus it is a great joy for a dying man to hear that Christ became a man and the Word of God became flesh.

---

[38] *Commentarium in Osee*, in Migne, ed., *PL*, vol. 25, 815ff.

You ought to turn the eye of your mind to this manhood of Christ, as did, with great longing, all the Fathers, who were no doubt aware that the world might not be saved in any other way but through the manhood of Christ. Indeed, there is no other name in heaven or on earth wherein we may be saved but the name of Christ. Salvation is from the Godhead, redemption from the manhood. If the divine is too high for you, grasp onto the human. That is what you are, that is also what Jesus is, namely a man, your redeemer, your intercessor and intermediary with God the Father. He died for you and arose again and ascended to heaven so that you might follow him and live with him for eternity. That you ought firmly to believe and boldly confess with your mouth, etc.

And later in the third chapter we read: Although such things would be enough for salvation, still there are also a number of outward signs which awake such faith in us and stir our hearts to devotion. The Christian order requires this and friends are consoled and take good hope from it. There is, for example, the sign of Christ's bitter suffering which Christians call a crucifix. The figure of a suffering man is painted or carved on a cross so that the dying man will be reminded of the passion of Christ. You ought humbly to grasp and devotedly venerate that same sign and thereby reflect on God, since although this bit of wood is neither God nor man, nevertheless it makes you mindful of him who is both true God and man, who helps you and gives the rest of us good hope for your salvation.[39] Thus Augustine, who also adds other and similar considerations.

See, worthy Germans, how it is not a new, but rather an old Christian custom and usage to put the crucifix into the hands of a dying man or hold it for him so that he does not forget the passion of Christ. For there are not always people at hand who can read a Gospel to him, and even if one read all four Gospels to him, all four only speak of the physical suffering of Christ—how he was betrayed, taken prisoner, led before the people, mocked, judged, and nailed to the cross and gave up his spirit for us poor sinners. What is this poor man Karlstadt babbling about, or who, beside the evil one, has inspired him to put obstacles in the way of men's salvation? Men who in their extreme need are much distracted and concerned because of

---

[39] *De visitatione infirmorum*, in Migne, ed., *PL*, vol. 40, 1147ff. Augustine was probably not the author of this tract.

their illness, because of their sins, because of their friends, because of worldly goods and other things that it would be no wonder that they would forget God and all his saints if they were not made mindful by outward signs and admonitions.[40]

KARLSTADT

And, second, I say that images in general are forbidden and prophets have preached against likenesses. (Habakkuk 2[:19]) God says: Woe to him who says to the wood, Wake up, etc.

EMSER

This and other prophets forbid images no more than God has forbidden them. That is to say, one shall not invoke them as gods or put any trust or hope in them. Therefore Micah calls them dumb images. Now our images may never be called dumb since they were never able to speak—deprivation presupposes an ability. So also the prophet Micah (5 [:13]) speaks only of the images of idols, which is why, before he begins to speak of images he says: I will cut off your witchcrafts and soothsayings [Micah 5:12]. That may in no way be understood as pertaining to our images, which we do not believe can foretell the future for us.

KARLSTADT

Fourth, I must tell the followers of Gregory the story of Bishop Epiphanius who in the time of Jerome removed a cloth from the church because an image of a saint or a crucified Christ was painted on it in violation of the scriptural prohibition.

EMSER

Not only did Epiphanius do that but also Serenus, the bishop of Marseilles, whom St Gregory chastised for doing such a thing, as we read in Book ix, cv of his letters, which has been taken into canon law.[41] Both these men, however, are pardoned inasmuch as the matter of images and the Scripture concerning images had not yet been taken up, explained, and interpreted by any council, just as, also, in a similar case, Cyprian, Donatus, and every other bishop gave the people communion in both kinds. Since then the Christian church has established the order which we now use and has explained the

---

[40] Allusions to the sacraments and the humanity of Christ are traditional in arguments defending images. The physical element was considered essential in the process of ascending to an understanding of the purely spiritual.

[41] *de conse. di 3,* and see 22 above and Karlstadt, notes 11 and 14.

meaning of Scripture. Now Karlstadt has also published a completely heretical book on the most worthy sacrament in both kinds, against which I would have written at length had I not been hindered by illness, and, in addition, had not been given to understand that my lord and most kind friend, the erudite and honourable Doctor Johannes Cochlaeus Dobeneck, dean of St Mary's Convent in Frankfurt, has undertaken to treat of the same material. Nevertheless, since I have no reason to believe otherwise than that the same Doctor is writing or has already written in Latin, and since I know that this heresy has spread widely in neighbouring lands and, in addition, that Eastertide is not far off, I will not shelter the poor, erring people from the Christian truth at the this point and will give but a little instruction so that their hearts will be at peace and they might the more fruitfully accommodate themselves to the most worthy sacrament according to Christian law.

The whole controversy centres, for the most part, on the words of John 6[:53]: Unless you eat my flesh and drink my blood you can have no life in you, etc. The heretics interpret these words in their own way and do not want to accept the teachings of the Christian churches. Yet Christ has not spoken of one kind or of two kinds and no one is forced by this text to the sacrament which has been instituted not in the form of flesh and blood but, rather, in the form of bread and wine. Now we find that in the Gospels Christ speaks of bread in twelve places and of wine not more than once. Thus we also discover that many times he blessed, broke, and distributed bread to the common people, as, for example, the two times in the wilderness. Again, he shared bread with the two disciples at Emmaus, and at other places, but he never blessed and gave wine to anyone except the twelve apostles when he transformed his gentle, holy body into both bread and wine and established this most worthy sacrament. Thus we read of no apostle who offered communion to the common people in both kinds, apart from what Paul writes to the Corinthians, whose custom he does not praise much. And he says that when he comes to them he would advise them to change their practice and establish a better order. Otherwise, wherever the holy twelve apostles and the other Christians have been gathered together, they have blessed, broken, and extended only bread to them, as we read in many chapters of the Acts of the Apostles.

In the second place, those who have taken communion in both kinds have discovered through daily practice that it is fraught with difficulties and that the red blood of Christ often and freely poured forth has frozen in winter and become mouldy or turned to vinegar in summer, which has been a great dishonour to the holy sacrament. And since, then, King Hezekiah smashed to pieces the brazen serpent, which God himself had ordered to be made and to be looked upon without sin, because it was misused by the Jews, as we read in Dist. 63, c. xxviii of the *Decretum,* why would then the Christian church not have the power to abolish entirely the one kind of communion in which so much difficulty and abuse is found, or, as I explained at length regarding this in my *Quadruplica,* which God himself instituted and the Christian church afterwards changed for honourable reasons and through the inspiration of the Holy Spirit.

In the third place, a great heresy grew out of this and the heretic Nestorius publicly taught and wrote that under the species of bread only the body without the blood, and under the species of the chalice only the blood without the body were transformed. For this reason not only the pope but the whole Christian church was moved to clarify this matter fully and have therefore decreed (as testimony to the firm belief that under either kind, namely the chalice and host, Christ is completely present in flesh and blood, body and soul, man and God) that not only the laity but also the priests (except at mass) should content themselves with one kind in which they receive Christ as fully as if they had taken both kinds.

What Karlstadt says in his heretical book about the two kinds, namely that there are two signs and therefore they must signify two things, is irrelevant. For Moses' burning bush, Aaron's flowering rod, and Gideon's bedewed fleece are three different signs, nevertheless they signify only one thing, namely the virgin birth of Mary without any male fluid, disarrangement or ruin of her virgin body. Because also he accuses not only the pope and the schools of higher learning but also all classes of society in the empire and the entire Christian church and causes the people to imagine that they should heed neither pope, nor emperor, nor princes, nor their councils, but rather follow Scripture and speak no more of the form of the bread or the wine, but only of the bread and wine, it is not to be supposed that this man who has lost his self-control, who, as he himself acknowledges, lost his brain and mind in a bleeding-basin, should direct or judge the understanding of Scripture. For so many excellent, learned, and holy men, of both the regular and secular clergy, have examined this issue in its length and breadth many times. Nor can it be believed that Christ would allow his beloved bride, the holy Christian church, to fall into such a terrible error and would have destroyed thereby so many people over such a long period of time. That would be unjust and sinful. Since I have no doubt that the erudite master and doctor, Johann Cochlaeus, whom I mentioned earlier, will treat and propound this subject in a masterful way, I wish to say no more here about it except that I want to have loyally warned all pious Christian hearts so that they do not allow themselves to be turned away in any way from the mother of the Christian churches, but believe and maintain only what she believes and maintains until they might receive more suitable arguments and instruction from our Christian teachers. For this much I know: that concerning this issue not one but many books will be written and are already under way. There- fore, stand fast in Christ, dearly beloved brothers and sisters, and do not let yourself be misled by this Beghardic heretic. For we want to present to you so much authoritative evidence that you shall see the truth not only with your eyes, but take it in your hands.[42]

To Epiphanius' and Serenus' treatment of images (to pick up where I left off) the saintly doctors answer that indeed they had zeal, but not in accord with knowledge. That is to say that although their intention may have been good, they were lacking in subtlety because they took the wrong attitude toward and misunderstood Scripture, which afterwards was explained and interpreted by the Christian churches.

### KARLSTADT
Scripture clearly states that God hates and is jealous of the images which the papists call books. And Isaiah writes (Isaiah 42[:17]): Those who trust in images shall be tormented with shame.

### EMSER
God does not hate our images, through which he is venerated, but the images of demons by which he is disgraced. And as if to point up the truth of this, the prophet Isaiah appended to the passage cited above—that is, they shall be tormented, etc.—this clause, namely:

---

[42] Karlstadt had supported the view that communion should be given to the laity in both kinds; his belief in the equality of laity and clergy before God bears an obvious relationship to his rejection of the notion of a Bible for the illiterate as a justification of images. Emser's long discussion of the Eucharist is, therefore, not out of place here, as it might at first seem.

They say to the images, you are our gods. We Christians do not say this, and that is something Karlstadt has deceitfully concealed and kept in his pen.

### KARLSTADT
Note that God caused an image to be made of fire or of a serpent (Num. 21[:9]). That image was inspired by God himself and was not created by a human mind. Nevertheless, Scripture praises King Hezekiah (2 Kings 18[:4]) for breaking up the same.

### EMSER
Johannes Teutonicus in his gloss on Dist. 63 of the *Decretum*, cited above, answers this argument in the following way. The reason why God caused this serpent to be erected was a temporary one. That is to say, only for so long as the Jews were bitten by snakes. As soon as this plague ceased, the image was no longer needed and there was no sin in breaking it up. But the reason for our images is eternal, for as long as the world exists we are obligated to venerate and worship God and the image reminds us of this. Therefore one ought not to remove or destroy them. But Rabbi Moses said that the Jews, because of the benefits they had received, believed the serpent by which they had been made healthy to be a god, just as they had the golden calf, and venerated it as if it were divine. Therefore Hezekiah destroyed and smashed it, together with other idolatrous images. The holy pope Stephan also used this reason in the already cited Dist. 63. But it should not be concluded from this that for this reason we also should smash our images, since we do not take them for idols or worship them.

### KARLSTADT
Our images do not come from God. Indeed they are forbidden by God.

### EMSER
That they are not forbidden has been sufficiently demonstrated above. But that they do not come from God, which is also the argument of the Arians, who despised painters because they represented God the Father in a grey beard although it was not the Father, but the Son who appeared in human form. St Athanasius answers this in a book of responses to Arian objections addressed to Bishop Lucifer and says that the painters have taken such images from the prophet Daniel to whom God appeared in that form. In Daniel 7 [:9] it is written: I kept looking until the thrones were set in place and the

old man ancient in days sat down, his robe was white as snow and his hair was like pure wool. And further on he says: And in a vision of the night I saw one come like to the Son of man, and he came to the Ancient of Days, who gave him power and honour and sovereignty. From this the Christian church and her painters have a good reason and cause to represent the Father as an old man and the Son as a young man. Thus Athanasius. How, then, can Karlstadt say that images do not come from God?

### KARLSTADT

You image-gluttons should mark well that God alone saves and no one else with him or beside him.

### EMSER

Who has ever understood, taught, or written differently than that God alone gives grace, help, consolation, salvation, and blessedness? As David says in Psalm 83[:12]: The Lord will give grace and glory, and in Psalm 120[:2]: My help cometh from Lord, which made heaven and earth. God alone is the font out of which originates and flows everything good in heaven and on earth. But you shall not conclude from this that we should not also seek the mediation and help of our beloved saints together with the Christian church and say, O Saint Peter or Saint Paul, pray for us. For although God can do everything for himself without any contrivances and toil, nevertheless he has always wanted, and has therefore so arranged it, that the powers of nature and the creatures he made should participate. God might indeed create all men, as he did Adam, from the earth and from nothing, yet he wants such things to happen by means of the sun and natural birth. As Aristotle says: Men and the sun generate man. Similarly, God himself might also protect and preserve us just as he created us. But, instead, he has given each and every man a personal angel who shall shield him and serve him. Thus, although God is the original source and font of all our help, he wills that we, as the lowest, shall be led to him by such means—that is, through the merit and mediation of the blessed saints—and come to him, as the highest, in accord with his divine wisdom. Not only nature teaches us that, but also Scripture. Luke 16[:9]: Make to yourselves friends from the Mammon of unrighteousness, etc. By these means it is God's intention to demonstrate to us the majesty of his power and the mightiness of his glory, that he has such strong and powerful servants who are called Powers and Virtues and he is called *Dominus exercituum*, that is, the Lord of the entire heavenly host. This host is not a detriment or injury to God's divinity, but, rather an honour, just as the more richly dressed and ornamented are the servants who accompany a prince arriving at an Imperial Diet, the more he is regarded as powerful and mighty. Thus, therefore, through the mediation of the beloved saints, God often gives us a gift which otherwise would not come our way. And it is by the extraordinary grace of God that we have refuge in and devotion to this or that saint because he loved God and God has honoured him in like measure. There is also no doubt that many men have been saved through the intercession of our beloved saints, as St Augustine proves in the *City of God*, Book 21, chapter 27. Therefore, he remains the font of all grace and help, but it flows nevertheless through the glorious cups and vessels of the company of the saints. This divine order the heretics, as blind and obdurate people, can neither see nor note. Therefore, they strive vigorously against the veneration of the blessed saints and their memorials and images. We, on the contrary, venerate them, so that thereby nothing is detracted from the veneration of God, but rather more is added.

### KARLSTADT

You want to venerate the saints in images, and [offer them] just that veneration which in their lives they shunned and forbade.

### EMSER

Paul, Barnabas, and the other apostles and the angel of Apocalypse 20, of whom Karlstadt speaks, only shunned divine veneration and forbade that anyone should pray to them as gods. St Augustine treats of this in *Contra Faustum*, Book 20, chapter 21 and the texts of Acts 14 and Apocalypse 19 and 20 clearly establish it. Now we Christians do not venerate the saints as gods, but as friends of God, as said above, and as we also, as Augustine says, venerate every pious man living. Therefore, Karlstadt has falsely accused us of doing that which the blessed saints have forbidden. But that he wants to cite in this regard the speech of Peter about the name Jesus in which alone we are saved, does not tally at all. For we are not arguing about names, but images, and none of us has ever said or written that images can save.

### KARLSTADT

What, however, will you say to the Bacchants' chant, St Christopher, such are your powers, etc.

EMSER

It is possible that the man who wrote this verse may have been a better Christian and, in addition, more learned than even Karlstadt. For St Cyril related to St Augustine (Epistle 206 on the miracles of St Jerome)[43] the story, true in every respect, of a monk who had an image of St Jerome in his cell. It was his established practice each day when he looked upon it to commend himself to the image and bow before it. When at nights he wanted secretly to pursue dissolute activities outside the cloister, this image miraculously prevented him for three nights, until, inspired by the Devil, he tore down the image and got rid of it. Why, therefore, should we not look willingly on the image of St Christopher or the images of other beloved saints, and day and night confidently trust ourselves to their intercession with God? They often appear visibly to their servants and come to their aid. In my first book against Luther's Reformation I related many stories about such things that are worthy of belief and the legends of the saints are full of them.

KARLSTADT

Because of this scandalous state of affairs you should counsel the belief that all images should be dragged down to the Devil.

EMSER

If everything that causes scandal should be dragged down to the Devil, then Karlstadt and Luther, who have made so many pious Christian hearts err and waver in their faith, must have fallen head-long to the Devil in the bottom of hell. Indeed, even the Holy Gospel might not escape hell, since so much scandal and heresy has come out of it and still does come daily. As I in my *Quadruplica* clearly showed, and the saintly old Simeon prophesied: Behold, this child is set for the fall and rising again of many in Israel (Luke 2[:34]). Therefore, one must not immediately cast something aside because some particular evil or foolish people misuse it or cause some scandal with it. For just as the bee draws honey and the spider poison from every plant, so there is nothing on earth so good that evil cannot pervert or misuse. But to the pure all things are pure, as the apostle says (Timothy 1[:5]).

---

[43] This letter, reproduced in Migne, ed., *PL*, vol. 33, 1127ff., was wrongly attributed to Cyril of Jerusalem; see *PG*, vol. 33, 1210, and *PL*, vol. 33, 1121.

KARLSTADT

You must also admit to me that many of the laity put much hope and trust in other images, etc.

EMSER

I do not admit in any way that these laity who hear sermons daily and in these and other cases receive good Christian instruction are so foolish that they place any trust or hope in images, but they bear love and devotion to images for the sake of the beloved saints. In order that they may understand that that is no idolatry, the holy Gregory writes as follows to Secundinus: We know very well that you do not request the image of our Saviour because you want to worship it as a God, but, rather, that through memory and by looking upon it you will become the more inwardly ardent in the love of Christ, just as we prostrate ourselves before the above-mentioned image not as before God, but rather, we pray to him whom the image represents to us, and thereby move beyond visible to invisible things. And just as his image on the crucifix makes us grieve through the contemplation of his sufferings, so we rejoice in other images, as of his birth and resurrection, because of the benefit we have received from those events. For this reason we now send to you by our deacon Dulcidius two panels, in one of which is an image of our Saviour and his Mother Mary. In the other are painted likenesses of the two apostles Peter and Paul.[44] Thus Gregory: From which we may take it that neither Saint Gregory nor the Christian church teaches us to put any sort of trust and hope in an image, but rather, in God, and that we do not worship images otherwise than the Christian councils mentioned above established and taught.

KARLSTADT

Look! You have permitted the laity to light candles before images of Sts Paul, Peter, and Barnabas and bring them offerings, etc.

EMSER

The heretic Vigilantius also wrote and complained against setting up candles. St Jerome answered him in a letter which begins *Multa in orbe monstra*. He says: Since God is venerated in his saints, what harm does it do to you or what do you lose if a pious person sets up a candle to honour a saint, although I certainly acknowledge myself that they do so out of well-meaning simplicity and might do some-

---

[44] Migne, ed., *PL*, vol. 72, 988 ff., esp. 991.

thing better.[45] Thus St Jerome. Wycliffe and Huss also complain that we burn out our eyes to the day with our candlelight.[46] And Erasmus of Rotterdam, although he chastises us and says in his *Enchiridion* or *Handbook of the Christian Knight*, that many seek something more for their own benefit than to honour the saints when they light a candle—such as the women who light candles to St Blasius to protect their pigs, to St Apollonius to make their wash white, or to another to insure that the beer is well brewed, and the like. Still, despite this, he does not condemn in general the lighting of candles or other outward ceremonies, but only the abuse of over reliance on these external things, in favour of which the inward, spiritual things, which concern us more, are omitted, for there is no offering more pleasing to God than a spirit grieving over its sin. So we can give our beloved saints no greater joy and do them no greater honour than to follow them diligently in their holy lives. The words of Erasmus are as follows: What then shall a Christian do? Shall he neglect the commandments of the Church? Shall he disdain the honourable traditions of the Fathers? Shall he condemn pious customs? On the contrary, if he is weak he shall observe them as necessary things, but if he is strong and perfect he shall observe them even more lest he harm a weak brother by his knowledge and kill him for whom Christ died. Physical works are not condemned, but invisible ones are preferred. Visible cults are not condemned, but God is pleased only by the invisible cult. And a little further on: You think a burning candle is a sacrifice. But David said an afflicted spirit is a sacrifice to God, etc. Thus the text of Erasmus.[47] Therefore, although it were perhaps better that one should give to poor and needy people the money one pays for unnecessary wax, nevertheless, when a man is so rich that he can do both without hurting himself, then I do not want to chastise [him], even as the angel did not chastise the three Marys because they had paid so much money for ointment, which, since the Lord was no longer in his grave, but was risen, was to no purpose and of no use.

---

[45] This is from *Contra Vigilantium*, in Migne, ed., *PL*, vol. 23, 353ff.

[46] Which is to say, we blind ourselves to daylight (i.e. the truth) by staring at banks of burning candles.

[47] *Enchiridion militis Christiani*, in Erasmus, *Opera Omnia* (Leiden, 1704), vol. 5, col. 37.

KARLSTADT

If you are such an erudite fellow, I beg you, in a friendly way, to tell me whether Paul, Peter, and Barnabas in person would have permitted us to place them on altars.

EMSER

Yes, the more the beloved saints shunned veneration in their lifetimes, the more worthy they are to be held in veneration after their death, as is written in Matthew 18[:4]: Every man who humbles himself shall be raised up. Indeed, God promised not only to place them on altars, but to give them charge of all his possessions (Matthew 24[:45ff.]). Moreover we place them thus on altars not as gods, but as friends of God, as St Paul himself says (Ephesians 2[:19]): You are now not strangers or foreigners, but fellow citizens with the saints, and of the household of God. Since, then, St Paul calls them members of God's household, why does Karlstadt want to eject and drive them out of the house of God?

KARLSTADT

O how evil it will be for those who, caught in the throes of death, cleave unto idols and bow and kneel before them.

EMSER

Neither in death nor in life do we fear images which can neither help nor harm us, unless one might chance to fall occasionally, as the old god from Schaffhausen toppled down and killed a man. But those whom they depict can no doubt protect and assist us at the end of our lives, as the Christian church sings—Mary, Mother of grace, Mother of mercy, protect us from the enemy, sustain us in death.

KARLSTADT

Now I come back to the beginning and turn to Isaiah, who says: They are of no use (Isaiah 44[:10]). Books are useful to readers. It follows that images are not books for the laity, contrary to what Gregory and his entire company say.

EMSER

I freely acknowledge that Karlstadt returns right to the beginning, for just as he deceitfully distorted Scripture at the beginning, so does he here. For the prophet in these words spoke not of our images, but rather, of idols and their images. The text is as follows: They that make a graven image are all of them vanity; and their delectable things shall not profit. And further on [verse 10]: Who has formed a god, or molten image that is profitable for nothing? But to suppose, and not to acknowledge it, that these words were also spoken of our images does not follow, as Karlstadt wants to conclude in the following false syllogism: Images are useless. Books are useful. Therefore images, are not books of the laity. For when in the second figure the major premise is a particular, nothing can be concluded. The same is true of mere affirmations.[48] Therefore, we do not accept this conclusion. Karlstadt then tries to demonstrate with better reason that images are not the books of the laity.

KARLSTADT

Listen to what Ezekiel says, you Gregorists and papists. If any renounces me and sets his heart upon idols, etc. (Ezekiel 14[:7]).

EMSER

Listen, you Arianist and Wycliffist, the text of the prophet reads as follows: Repent, and turn yourselves from your idols [Ezekiel 14:6]. And a little further on: For every one......which separateth himself from me, and setteth up his idols in his heart.....[Ezekiel 14:7]. Why do you then turn words spoken of idols onto our images and falsify the Scripture of the Holy Spirit? Have you not perpetrated the crime of fraud by doing this, or even committed a sacrilege?

KARLSTADT

Hear what follows in Ezekiel 14[:9]. If a prophet errs, I, the Lord, have made him err and will destroy him from the midst of my people.

EMSER

Mark these words yourself, for they have been written about you and other heretics.

KARLSTADT

If a man knows the commandment and will of God, he should follow it strictly and listen neither to angels, nor to saints, nor to prophets.

---

[48] Emser's comment on Karlstadt's syllogism reads, "Quia in secunda figure maiore existente particulari nihil sequitur. Similiter ex meris affirmationibus." It is difficult to make sense of the first sentence because of the syntax, but what it seems to amount to is refusal to accept the major premise as universal—i.e. that *all* images are useless—and to insist that it is particular—i.e. *some* images are useless. For the definition and discussion of the second figure, see Artistotle, *Prior Analytics*, I, 5.

## EMSER

There is no one who knows the will of God so completely that he does not also need the counsel, teachings, and instruction of the Christian church. For although Paul received his gospel from Christ himself, as he acknowledges in Galatians 1, nevertheless he did not want to preach without the instruction, advice, knowledge, and will of the other apostles who were at that time in Jerusalem (Gal. 1 and 2). By contrast Semeas allowed himself to be deceived by the lies of the false prophets, and that was his failing. Therefore, St John warned us to test whether the spirit is from God or not (1 John 4[:1]): Believe not every spirit. The stories of Nadab and Abihu do not have anything to do with images, but rather teach the laity that they ought not to presume upon and arrogate priestly authority. But when Balaam said that there were no images in Jacob and idols in Israel (Num. 23) he spoke of the images of idols only, otherwise he would have been lying, for already the cherubim of the tabernacle and the brazen serpent were daily displayed before the Jews (Num. 21).

## KARLSTADT

If someone comes and says that images teach and instruct the laity just as books do the learned, answer: God has forbidden me to use images, etc.

## EMSER

Regarding this and similar fables, it has been sufficiently demonstrated and shown above that God has not forbidden our images. When John says that God is a spirit and we must worship him in spirit and not in images, we agree, since we do not worship God in images, but in the presence of images are mindful of him alone, thereby awaken our spirits. The statement of Isaiah (44): Your foolish and senseless heart worships them, etc., is not about our images, but about idols, as we have often heard. But what John says about how we must all be students of God, concerns not only the laity with their images, but also the learned with their books. For if God does not touch and attract our hearts, neither book nor image can help.

## KARLSTADT

Whenever I want to have an outward admonition and reminder, I should desire the kind of reminder which Scripture indicates. I would much rather fall with horse and cart into sore tribulation and distress than come to an image, etc.

EMSER

Perhaps Karlstadt means the cart with which he fell into the mud at Leipzig.[49] And not only did he come to grief in that same cart and through Doctor Eck, but he also suffered mockery and cat-calls enough from all the listeners (because he did not debate but read from cards) when he wanted otherwise to become enlightened and according to the text of Isaiah 28[:19] such vexation might have given him understanding. But, as the prophet Ezekiel says: He who God makes to err and the Devil blinds by God's decree, cannot be helped by either inner or outer warnings. For he is in himself hardened and callused, as we fear may have almost happened to Karlstadt. The passages from Isaiah 2 and 13, and Micah 5 speak only of idols and not of our images. Even if Karlstadt produces a whole sack full of texts about idols, he cannot thereby prove that all images are forbidden, since otherwise God himself would not have commanded Moses and Solomon to make and set up images.

KARLSTADT

A Christian therefore can understand that pictures should not be called books. Books instruct. But images cannot instruct, as Habakkuk says in chapter 2[:17]. Is it possible that it can teach? And further on he writes: From all this everybody can recognize that Gregory the pope has indeed taught in a popish, that is to say, unchristian, way when he gives pictures to the laity as books.

EMSER

Habbakuk also speaks of the images of idols, which the heathen do not use as signs, but as actual gods: Therefore they say to them, Wake up! or Stand up! as the text says. Since, however, we Christians use our images only as signs, and each sign is made to signify or indicate something, as a drawing of a hoop or circle in front of a house teaches or shows me that beer or wine is sold there, how can then anyone who has a drop of understanding deny that our images teach and show us, just like books, what this or that saint suffered, or why St Lawrence is depicted with a grill, or St Catherine with a wheel, or St Sebastian with a pillar. For they bring home to us their sufferings and martyrdoms not less than if we had read about them

---

[49] Emser refers to the accident which threw Karlstadt from his wagon as he entered Leipzig in June 1518 for the debate with Eck. See Sider, *A. Bodenstein von Karlstadt*, 71.

in books. Why then does Karlstadt accuse and slander St Gregory and all the popes [by saying] that they have taught in an unchristian way in these matters? O holy Father Gregory, how long can you bear this insult of the heretics? I would almost like to say to you, wake up, stand up, and defend your honour yourself, for the obdurate people will never attend to me.

### KARLSTADT

Scripture compares images and idols to whores and says in many places that the godless commit whoredom with images as whores do with dissolute men.

### EMSER

All the passages of Scripture which Karlstadt adduces speak of the worshippers of idols or (according to the spiritual sense) of the heretics, as Jerome teaches, and not of our images. And that it is true is demonstrated by the text of Ezekiel 6[:4]: And I will cast down your slain men before your idols. Again, Ezekiel 16[:16]: And of thy garments, thou didst take, and deckedst thy high places. Moreover, thou hast taken thy sons and thy daughters, whom thou hast borne unto me, and these hast thou sacrificed unto them to be devoured [Ezekiel 16:20]. Again, Hosea 2[:16–17]: And it shall be at that day, saith the Lord, that thou shalt call me Ishi; and shalt call me no more Baali. For I will take away the names of Baalim out of her mouth. Therefore, one cannot conclude that our images may be called whores and the churches whorehouses, as that presumptuous, shameless man without any fear of God dares to describe them.

### KARLSTADT

We call the image of the Crucified One a lord god and sometimes say that it is the Lord Jesus and venerate it as if it were Christ himself. We say also that this image is St Sebastian, that one St Nicholas, etc. The wicked popes and foolish monks have brought us to this.

### EMSER

That we give to images the names of those whose shape and figure they represent is a tired refrain and is masterfully answered by Augustine above. The divine honour and reverence we offer the crucifix is in no way offered to the wood or other materials, but to God himself. But whether in this matter the popes or monks, or Karlstadt himself has written as a wicked, crazy simpleton, I will let the Christian churches decide. That God is a jealous God, together with the claims in Exodus 20, Hosea 2 and 7, Isaiah 1 and 44, is to be understood to mean that God can tolerate none next to or beside him who wants to be as much and as greatly venerated as he; as Lucifer wanted to be. For as Augustine and Lactantius demonstrate, it is not possible for there be two Gods. But towards his own, who are willing to be subordinate to him and do not wish to challenge him, he is not an angry God. Therefore he says (Isaiah 42[:8]) not that he would take away or begrudge the saints their proper veneration. But, rather, he says I will not surrender my divine veneration to another, that is, to the idols. Karlstadt also falsely says that Deut. 17[:2–5] condemns all those who carve or worship images, for the text speaks only of those who serve and worship alien gods, such as the sun or moon. Since Karlstadt saw this chapter, why then has he not also taken to heart the words about him and others who insult popes or priests which follow immediately after: Whoever rises up in court and will not be obedient to the priest who at all times administers the office of God, he shall die by the judgement and law of the judge, so that the people who see such things are afraid and no one so easily puffs himself arrogantly against the priest [Deut. 17:12–13]. Now, Karlstadt, since you have insulted and slandered so many of God's popes and priests, both dead and living, and still daily insult and slander them, say for yourself whether you have not earned a sentence of death a thousand times over.

### KARLSTADT

Now I want and shall say to all pious Christians that all those who stand in awe before pictures have idols in their hearts.

### EMSER

Let him who is afraid don armour. Perhaps Karlstadt thinks that because he trembled and was in awe before images, and, as he says, was concerned that some devil's dummy might injure him, that we are also accustomed to stand in awe of images. But we more love and venerate them, than fear them. So Karlstadt has not yet escaped the fool-eater[50] before he trots out for us passages from Judges 6 and 2 Kings 17 which are not about images, but, rather, about alien gods: that we shall not stand in awe of them, etc.

### KARLSTADT

From the texts quoted above it follows that Christians should strictly observe God's counsel, will, and command and no longer

---

[50] I.e. the bogeyman.

permit images. And this notwithstanding the old evil custom and the pestilential teaching of priests that they [images] are the books of laity. For God has prohibited the making and keeping of images.

### EMSER

Indeed, when Karlstadt first irrefutably proves that God forbids the making or keeping of all images, and, again, that the old custom of the churches and the teachings of the holy Fathers and the councils is pestilential, then we could send images packing. It has, however, not happened so far, so I think we will be wanting to bake flat cakes several times before he brings that about.[51]

### KARLSTADT

Thus we have documented and given honest proof of our first two articles through the testimony of the Holy Spirit, etc.

### EMSER

So arrogant is this man that he can even attribute lies to the Holy Spirit. Yet it is not the Holy Spirit but rather Karlstadt himself who falsely claims that God said through Jeremiah that images pollute or stain his house. For the prophet does not speak of images in general, of which there were many in the Temple of Solomon without transgression, but spoke rather of the two idols Baal and Molech, as the letter of the text clearly indicates. It reads as follows: But they set their abominations in the house, which is called by my name, to defile it. And they built the high places of Baal, which are in the valley of the son of Hinnom, to cause their sons and their daughters to pass through the fire unto Molech [Jer. 32:34–35]. From this text it clearly appears that the Holy Spirit does not bear witness to Karlstadt's lies, and that the said Karlstadt has not proved thereby his two articles.

### KARLSTADT

The third article flows naturally from the passages of Scripture which have been cited. Nevertheless, I want to adduce particular testimony from Scripture. Thus shall you deal with them, says God (Deut. 7[:5]): You shall overthrow their altars. You shall smash their images. You shall hack down their groves, etc.

---

[51] So-called flat cakes were eaten at Eastertide, so that the sense here is that it will be many years before Karlstadt proves anything.

EMSER

This passage proves nothing against our images but, rather, against the images of the seven heathen kings and their altars, as the text which follows makes clear: Thine eyes shall have no pity upon them, neither shalt thou serve their gods, for that will be a snare unto thee [Deut. 7:16]. Karlstadt's claim that we Christians have no divine altars but only heathen or human is also not demonstrated by the text of Exodus 20, as he proudly claims. Moreover, since he himself earlier called divine the altars which Noah, Jacob, Moses, and others set up to God, why should not the Christian altars, which we now set up for the veneration of the same God of old, also not be called divine? Indeed, the holy Dionysius never calls our altars anything but divine. But how could we have a better testimony against Karlstadt than that even the holy Paul did not remove the altar in Athens which was dedicated to the unknown God, nor smash it, but, rather, gave his first sermon about it: that it was the altar of the very God he wanted to proclaim (Acts 17). Augustine deals with this in the book on baptism addressed to Constantine.

KARLSTADT

The secular authorities should remove images and subject them to the judgement to which Scripture has subjected them.

EMSER

If our images should not be judged in any other way than they are in Scripture, then they would long ago have been left in peace, since Scripture has not touched on them with a single word, much less forbidden them.

KARLSTADT

I should also have hoped that the living God, having inspired in us a healthy desire for the removal of images, might have seen the task to its conclusion.

EMSER

Indeed, you should certainly believe, were it God's work, that it would have long since been done. Since, however, whoever destroys images extinguishes thereby also thoughts of God and the saints, and God does not wish us to forget him or his elected, you can do, write, make, and order as long as you want and nothing will ever come of it and you will receive nothing from it but mockery and abuse. I pledge you my oath to that.

About Hezekiah, why he is praised in Scripture was discussed above. But in regard to Karlstadt's wish that our kings and princes were as pious as the Jewish kings, it seems to me beyond all doubt that we have much more pious kings and princes than the the Jews. And the fact that King Josiah took the idol Baal out of the temple and burned it is not conclusive proof that the pope together with the entire priesthood should be subordinated to the secular authorities, since there is now another arrangement regarding the priesthood than in the Old Law, as I have written in my *Quadruplica*, where I showed why Moses spoke of a priestly kingdom and Peter of a kingly priesthood, etc.

We also do not concede in anyway to Karlstadt that our fathers were Amorites or our mothers Hittites, and that we should not follow them in that which is Christian and praiseworthy, for they were all pious Christian people, and may God permit that we do not become worse than the fathers, as Horace laments: Our parents' age, worse than our grandfathers', has brought us forth less worthy and destined soon to yield an offspring more wicked.[52]

### KARLSTADT

Certain image-kissers say: The Old Law forbids images; the New does not. And we follow the New, not the Old.

### EMSER

Our images are forbidden neither by the New or the Old Testament. And we know very well that Christ did not suspend or discard the Old Law, but, rather, fulfilled and illuminated it. Therefore it is idle prattle and empty words that Karlstadt wants here, from a false assumption, to drag erroneously [into the argument].

Finally, Karlstadt undertakes to harmonize Moses and Paul with the first Epistle to the Romans. There it is written that they have exchanged the splendour of the immortal for the likeness not only of a mortal man but also of birds, of four-footed and creeping animals, etc. But just as previously Karlstadt misunderstood Moses, who in Exodus 20 wrote only of images which had been worshipped as idols, so the poor man also does not understand Paul rightly, who, just as Moses, speaks only of likenesses and figures which the heathens have worshipped as gods, as the Egyptians worshipped

---

[52] Horace, *Odes* iii, 6, 46–48, adapted from the translation of C. E. Bennett, Loeb Classical Library (London, 1914).

storks, the Romans the geese who awakened them at night on the Capitoline hill, and the Babylonians the dragon which Daniel slew. And Jeroboam also erected images of calves in Samaria, and various heathens have worshipped ravens, and in this land one animal and in that land another, as St Ambrose has clearly explained and interpreted the words of St Paul [in his commentary on] the first Epistle to the Romans. Paul spoke also in other Epistles not of images but of idols, in all of which passages the worship of idols is expressly named as one thing among others which excludes us from the kingdom of God. Thus Moses and Paul are indeed in agreement, but not in the sense which Karlstadt wrongly understands and sets out, but rather in the way that the holy Fathers have interpreted Scripture for us and the Christian councils have established. With this, convinced that I have refuted Karlstadt's three heretical propositions and proved my own, and trusting that there is little or nothing at all in his book that remains unanswered, I set out my conclusions for the edification and enlightenment of the entire Christian church and every reasonable, God-fearing reader.[53]

Nevertheless, I do not want to defend or excuse in any way in this book the abuses of images which go on in our times, abuses which do not please me at all and are not in accord with the opinion of the holy Fathers. I will briefly indicate what these abuses are.

First, our ancestors, as I have seen in many old cloisters and collegiate churches, placed quite simple images in the churches. This was not done because of any decline of art (for in earlier times there were no doubt capable painters, although they were not so common as they are now) but for two other reasons, namely that the people preferred to give the vast amounts of money which we spend on pictures today, often paying six, seven, eight, and even a thousand guilders for a single panel, to the blessed poor. The other reason is that the more artfully images are made the more their viewers are lost in contemplation of the art and manner in which the figures have been worked. We should turn this contemplation from the images to the saints which they represent. Indeed, many are transfixed before the pictures and admire them so much that they never reflect on the

---

[53] Emser follow here a medieval tradition, also to be found in Thomas Aquinas' *Summa,* that the pagans venerated animals and other natural forms like the sun and moon, and that this was another basic difference between pagan idolatry and the Christian use of images.

saints. Therefore, it would be far better for us to follow the old custom and have simple pictures in the churches so that expense would be spared and God and the saints would be venerated more than in this new manner which we now have.

The second abuse is that the painters and sculptors make images of the beloved saints so shamelessly whorish and roguish that neither Venus nor Cupid were so scandalously painted or carved by the pagans. The holy Fathers would not have approved of this. For when we look at the old picture, it is a honourable thing and all the limbs are covered so that no one can conceive from it an evil desire or thought. Therefore, I believe that God will now punish the painters and forbid them the practice of their craft if they do not abandon these scandalous ways. For it would be far better to lay such improper and shameless images in the fire than to set them up on altars or in the churches. Indeed, even secular pictures should not be painted so shameless and naked, for they greatly stimulate the desires of the flesh, sin, and scandal. But that is the fault of a perverted world, not of images, and therefore not all images should be removed.[54]

The third abuse is that we are too ready to burst in and offer candles and other things to images. Thus one should not believe in miracles or other signs unless they have been examined, evaluated, and authenticated by pope and bishops. That monks and priests foolishly allow such things in their churches is inexcusable and one is afraid that they, for the sake of their own advantage, are more diligent regarding their images (so that the churches will be decorated and have great congregations) than they are in caring about the living images, which are the souls of men who were created in God's image (Gen.1[:26]). These and similar misuses are not, in my opinion, to be defended, but, rather, all the leaders and prelates of the Church ought to establish and enforce, in accord with God's will, those rules governing the use of images which were established by the holy Fathers and the councils. Then the heretics will not find reason so mercilessly to rebuke, burn, and hack images to pieces as has happened in various places and perhaps because of the abuses

---

[54] The criticism of licentious images had already been expressed in the previous century, as Eck notes (see Eck, note 36), but this was never an important issue for the Reformers.

mentioned above. For where one uses images as they were used and set up in earlier times, they are, as I said in the beginning, praiseworthy, Christian, and divine. They cannot justly be removed, for had God wanted them removed, the matter would not have been reserved for Karlstadt, for much serious effort has gone into this matter. Moreover, Scripture has also never forbidden images, as even Christ did not say the image of the emperor on the coin which the Jews gave to him should be expunged, because the emperor's image was struck there not as an idol but as an emperor, and Scripture only forbids images of idols, as I have convincingly demonstrated above.

From all this any reasonable man can judge for himself that since Christ did not begrudge the emperor veneration and did not forbid us to place his image on coins or to have among us other memorials and objects of veneration, how much more would he not begrudge such veneration to his saints. Therefore, I am afraid that this business of the heretics began solely because they wanted to tear from our hearts all veneration and regard for our beloved saints. They have already written that the saints cannot help us at all nor pray for us, and thereby hope that they would talk us out of serving the saints. But since we do not heed them and they note the images of the saints that stand daily before our eyes do not allow us to forget our beloved saints, they want to remove their images. Not only Karlstadt, but also his teacher Luther. For although Luther now preaches and scolds because his monks have so precipitously taken images away (that is, they should have held back the jack for a while longer and abided until the Imperial Diet in Nuremberg was over) nevertheless, he cannot conceal his own heretical heart and himself preaches that one should talk people out of their need for images and then gradually, over a period of time, remove them.[55] But I have no doubt that pious Christians will not heed his brilliant and polished speech. The Christian church will also not permit that. For since Luther allows his own charming features to be painted and publicly displayed, why should the church not treasure and venerate images of the beloved saints?

But if you, Karlstadt, are not pleased with this answer and want to respond to it, I will have you first forewarned that I have at home

---

[55] Emser recognized that Luther, and not Karlstadt, was really responsible for all the disruptions taking place in Germany. For Luther's view of images, see Christensen, *Art and the Reformation in Germany*, 42ff.

two boxes or trunks. In the one I am in the habit of putting words of abuse, and Luther and his followers have filled it entirely. In the other I put good rejoinders and refutations of my arguments. It is quite empty. Therefore, if you want to write something against me, spare the abusive words, for I already have enough and do not know how to store more, and bring forth something substantial. Then I will respond to you in the same way. But I will give you some good advice. Stay home and recant your heretical book, for as it is, you have enough to answer for. May God have mercy on you so that you may better know, venerate, and be thankful to him and to his saints than you have up to now. That I will not begrudge you from the bottom of my heart, and I hope by virtue of my little book you will become a good Christian again, learn to interpret Scripture correctly, and note how scandalously the books of Wycliffe and Huss have led you astray. Here I will let matters stand for now.

Praise, honour, and thanks be to God and the entire heavenly host forever and ever. May the author be granted eternal forgiveness for his sins, and may God grant his mercy and eternal salvation to all pious Christian hearts. Amen.

# On Not Removing Images
## of Christ and the Saints

by Johannes Eck

Wherein it is argued that images of Christ and the saints should not be removed, and against the heresy of Felix of Urgel[1] which was condemned under Charlemagne and rose again under Charles V.

To the most worthy Bishop of Brixen, Sebastian Sprenger,[2] from Johannes Eck:

I remember, most reverend Bishop, that when I was returning from Rome, I digressed from my way to see you and we deliberated over the veneration of the saints. Then, when I arrived in Ingolstadt, I discovered that the Lutheran faction, while scheming all sorts of evil, had in addition removed crucifixes and images of the Virgin and the saints. And so I immediately resolved that before undertaking a more serious study, I would set out in a brief treatise the reason for the use of images. Now I have striven to publish that work desired by many under your auspices and dedicated to your name. For although the gifts of your intellect, your exceptional learning, and distinguished virtues of spirit would deserve greater things (you who previously, while earning pay as a teacher of literature in our university at Ingolstadt, climbed steadily through the grades of offices to pontifical rank as your merits deserve), so great is your modesty and your sense of humanity that you will not disdain this trifle from a

---

[1] While Emser mentions Wycliffe and Huss as the forerunners of the iconoclasts and calls this heresy Beghardic, Eck prefers to focus on Felix of Urgel and to call iconoclasm the Felician heresy, perhaps because Felix was condemned at the Council of Frankfurt of 794, while the iconoclastic tendencies of Lollards, Hussites, and Beghards had never been condemned by Church councils.

[2] On Sebastian Sprenger, see Iserloh, "Die Verteidigung," 76.

well-meaning friend. Therefore, I present this work to you and through you to the world. Hail, most vigilant Bishop. Ingolstadt, 8 July, year of the Lord 1522.

In thy name, O sweet Jesus.

## The Preface

With so many heretical disturbances appearing everywhere in the Christian world, who would not judge these latest times to be those foretold by St Paul, when men will love themselves, be covetous, boastful, proud, blasphemers, and disobedient to their parents (2 Tim. 3[:2])? Every day we see new heretical doctrines against the Church, against the saints, and against God himself spreading out from the north (whence every evil comes) and from other parts of the world (Jer. 1[:14]). And because preachers of evil attract like-minded people, they collect corrupt followers (2 Tim. 4[:3?]). Since they do not hold up sound doctrine, but, rather, gather around themselves, for their own selfish purposes, masters with wanton ears and turn away from hearing the truth, it is as useless to preach something to them as it is to tell a deaf man stories. Consequently, in the present circumstances, I do not intend to write for those hardened and obstinate men, having learned from the apostle (Titus 3[:10]) to avoid the heretical man after he has been rebuked once and then a second time, knowing that man of this kind is morally lost: for it is clear that those monsters Luther, Karlstadt, Melanchthon have descended to the lowest level of evil, and therefore they regard evil as nothing.[3] Rather, I have decided to write here, for the consolation of faith, a treatise for the little ones so that they will not, in their simplicity, be deceived by these wolves concerning the destruction of images of the crucified Christ and of saints—seeing that they are now striving zealously towards this goal, covering over their wolf-like hearts with skin of sheep, as though the well-established tradition of the Church handed down to us by the apostles was a particular kind of idolatry and superstition, something that the sons of Belial impiously and blasphemously assert. If the great and good God helps me through his merciful grace, I will clearly demonstrate this. But I

---

[3] In one of the editions, there is a marginal reference at this point to Prov. 18, but we find nothing in this proverb which relates to the text.

warn you, dear reader—may God love you and the saints protect you—you should bury your personal feelings and fix the eyes of your mind on the truth itself and listen to your mother, the bride of Christ, the holy Church, and observe her decrees.

## Chapter I. Through the incarnation of the Word, the invisible God was made visible and capable of being represented.

The reader, however, should not expect that I will discuss the veneration of the saints and their relics, although the heretics rage extraordinarily about this with their usual rashness. For St Jerome abundantly repaid their trickery when he conquered and destroyed that great monster Vigilantius (Augustine, *The City of God*, bk 22, ch. 8), who was full of these kinds of heresies, with the spiritual sword of holy Scripture. I will only endeavour to show and demonstrate that the custom of the whole Church of displaying images of the crucifix and the saints is good and that whoever believes that images must be taken down and removed is an enemy of the Catholic faith, infected with heresy, and cut off from the communion of the faithful.

Although the authority of the whole Church and the custom of the most esteemed men through so many centuries should be sufficient to prove this, we will, nevertheless, for the consolation of the faithful, begin in the distant past, with John of Damascus, who said: Because God by his own nature is invisible and incorporeal and uncircumscribable, he likewise could not be represented, since a form is delimited and circumscribed by lines. Therefore, it would have been a great foolishness to represent the Divinity or to produce a corporeal image of him; and this is probably the one reason why the use of images was comparatively rare and less commonly employed in the Old Testament, about which we will speak more fully at the end of this work. But when the fullness of time was come, God sent forth his Son, made of a woman, made under the Law (Gal. 4[:4]), and the ineffable Word was made flesh and dwelt among us (John 1[:14]) and was made in the likeness of men (Phil. 2[:7]). Not, then, in the outward appearance of a man, as he appeared to Abraham; not as he appeared to the prophets; but in truth made a man for our salvation. For God took a body that was neither imaginary, nor celestial, nor made of air, as the impious, heretical Manicheans, Valentinians, and Apollinarians believed, but rather true anointed God and true man dwelling on the earth among men. He performed miracles; suffered; was crucified; died and was buried; then rising from the dead, he ascended into heaven. All these things were done in reality and likewise seen and written down by men.[4] It is easy for the faithful, when this explanation is considered, to understand the arrangement by which what could not be represented before can now be given a form. It is because the invisible has been made visible. For just as Christ presented himself before human eyes, so also the painter of that time was able to show to human sense and vision what he had seen. And just as in every church there is placed an image of the crucified Christ in a visible form, so also Mother Mary, the apostles, and the Jews saw with their physical eyes the passion of Christ and how he was affixed to the cross. Clearly, now, it is foolish for someone to argue that the use of images was not permitted under the Old Law and therefore should be rejected under the Law of Grace. But we will say more concerning this at the end of this work.[5]

## Chapter II.  Christ was the first authority for use of sacred images; concerning Abgar and Veronica.

Our Saviour, anticipating the cunning of his evil enemy and the rashness of these men, was the first to demonstrate the use of images at the time when he began his actions and his teaching. John of Damascus mentions this in the fourth book of his *Theology*, where he writes: A certain story is told, [according to which] Abgar, king of the city of Edessa, sent an artist to paint an exact likeness of the Lord. But the artist was unable to do this because of the resplendent glow of his face. Therefore, Christ pressed a cloth to his divine and life-giving face and left his image on it. This he sent to Abgar, who was eagerly awaiting it.[6] Eusebius of Cesarea, that most diligent

---

[4] Eck appears here to paraphrase from John of Damascus' first oration (tr. Anderson, 18) and ultimately from the Apostolic Creed. For the work of John of Damascus on images, see Introduction, note 32.

[5] That the incarnation made the law forbidding a representation of God obsolete was a principle stated by John of Damascus, who is quoted here by Eck. By emphasizing that Christ was also a man, Eck implies that a refusal to represent him is tantamount to dismissing his humanity.

[6] The original has: "Fertur quaedam hystoria: quod dominus Abgaro Edessenorum civitatis regi: qui pictorem miserat ut domini similem pingeret imaginem: etc." It is hard to restore a text obviously corrupted, and such that no indication is given on the original syntax; the translatin given here aims at rendering the meaning of the story. (See the original passage in John of Damascus, *De fide Orthodoxa*, in Migne, ed., *PG*, vol. 94, 1174; John of Damascus reports the

ecclesiastical writer, records this story, among many others, in the last three chapters of the first book of his *History of the Church*. He testifies there that he obtained the stories from the public archives of the city of Edessa, in which Abgar had reigned, where he found the texts among some ancient papers recording the deeds of King Abgar. In order to make his account the more trustworthy, Eusebius tells of a number of letters written by both Christ and Abgar which had been sent through the messenger Ananias. For the most gentle Jesus wrote to King Abgar to say that although he could not come to him in person, as he was fulfilling the work to which he was destined by his Father, he would, after his ascension, send one of his disciples to free him of the troubles of his illness. And, in fact, St Thomas did send St Thaddeus, one of the seventy disciples, who restored Abgar to health and instructed him in the right Christian faith. Thus we have the Saviour himself as authority for the use of images.[7] With such a prince and leader, the Church can be completely secure in the use of images as opposed to those most perfidious, cerberian dogs who bark at the most solemn rituals of the Church. The image sent to Abgar is preserved today in the church of St Bartholomew in Genoa.

Much celebrated also is the story of Veronica, who proffered to our Lord in his most bitter passion, labouring in the agony of death, a cloth with which to wipe the sweat of his suffering. The Saviour, about to depart from this world and desiring to leave a visible image of himself and to those dear to him, impressed on the cloth the image of his holy face and gave it back to Veronica. This image is preserved today in Rome and is most piously exhibited to the pilgrims who come to see it on certain special days. It is a sign of human rashness that the use of images in the Church is being attacked, although this use has had our Lord as its author and creator.[8]

## Chapter III. The use of images was given to us by the apostles and St Luke.

Moreover, just as our Saviour himself created the first images in the Church, so also the veneration of images of the crucifix, of the Virgin who gave birth to God, and of the other saints and servants of Christ is believed to have been advanced by the apostles. Now the holy

---

story from Evagrius, *Historia*, xxvii).

[7] See Emser, note 14.

[8] These are the same stories reported by Emser. See Emser, note 14.

tradition of the apostles should not be denied out of hand because it cannot be found in writings, for many things like this are kept the way they are received by tradition, as I will discuss at greater length elsewhere. Here it will suffice to report what the Greek author, John of Damascus, concludes from a parallel circumstance, viz., that it is not by chance that we worship facing east, but by the tradition of the Fathers and the apostles, while by contrast, as we know from Ezekiel (8[:16]), the Jews of the Old Law worshipped facing west by divine command. This and other apostolic traditions of the sort were transmitted orally and without writing.

We can easily understand this from the letter St Paul wrote to the Corinthians about many things concerning the communion of the eucharistic sacrament (1 Cor. 11[:20ff.]). At the end he added: I will arrange the rest when I come. He was, thus, about to make arrangements with the Corinthians in addition to what he had said in both letters to them. And at the beginning of the same chapter (1 Cor. 11[:2]) he praises them for the observance of their traditions, saying: I praise you, brothers, because in everything you remembered my words; and you kept my rules just as I handed them to you. And even more explicitly, in writing to the Thessalonians (2 Thess. 2[:15]) he teaches that certain things are known through writings, other things through the word of the apostles, saying: Therefore, brothers, stand fast and hold to the traditions which you have been taught, whether by word, or our epistle.[9]

All the above is confirmed by the fact that St Luke, a disciple of the Lord and an evangelist, created an image of the Blessed Virgin and painted it on some panels. One such image is piously preserved in the Franciscan church of S. Maria in Aracoeli. Another is in the cathedral church of the Bavarian duchy in Freising.[10] This image of the Virgin Mary appeared to the Emperor Louis IV in a dream and ordered him to erect a monastery in the very place indicated to him. This, indeed, the Catholic prince did most piously accomplish at the place which had been determined, always carrying with him to his intended destination the image on his sleeve, although it was heavy.

---

[9] Eck, like Emser, holds to the Catholic dogma that Christian doctrine is based on Scripture *and* tradition. It has to be said, however, that also John of Damascus insists on the tradition in the first oration on images, ch. 23 (tr. Anderson, 31).

[10] In the 16th century there were several Byzantine paintings in Europe that were believed to have been painted by St Luke.

Etcetera. Nor, throughout the centuries until today, has any artisan or any other kind of man been able to determine or discover the kind of material of which the image is made.

The Old Testament also was not without images as is most clearly shown to us by God's command in Exodus (25[:18–20]), when he says to Moses: You shall also make two cherubim of gold, of beaten work, at the two ends of the mercy seat; one cherub has to be on the one end and other cherub on the other end. And they shall conceal both sides of the mercy seat by stretching forth their wings and covering the mercy seat with their faces looking at one another over the mercy seat. See how clearly sacred Scripture describes the two images that had to be made. In a similar way it also says that Solomon placed many images in the temple.[11]

## Chapter IV. That the use of images is an ancient custom of the Church is proven from the works of Eusebius, Augustine, Jerome, and Ambrose.

Further, one does not need to say with how much devotion Constantine the first, the most Christian emperor, honoured the image of the cross shown to him from heaven, because this story is better known to the faithful than the story of Troy. Under that excellent prince loftier churches were built, festivities were frequently celebrated by the Christians, and new churches were dedicated.[12] Under him the priesthood, the ministry, and everything pertaining to religious observance was made resplendent by his great favours, as Eusebius testifies, and also St Augustine in the third book of his *On Visiting the Ill* with regard to that laudable ritual, namely presenting the cross and image of the crucified Christ to those about die,[13] a custom which all true Christians observe to this day. It is well to make special note of what Augustine has to say: Indeed, the mysteries of this true cross of the Christians are something like a venerable monument, which

---

[11] That God ordered the cherubim to be carved on the mercy seat was traditionally believed to be proof that God accepted images. See, on the cherubim, John of Damascus' first oration, ch. 15 (tr. Anderson, 22) and on the images in the temple, idem., second oration, ch. 15 (tr. Anderson, 62). On the issue, see also Karlstadt, note 11.

[12] The various churches built by Constantine are described in detail by Eusebius in his *Life of Constantine.*

[13] See Karlstadt, note 13, and Emser, note 39.

from the image of the cross itself they call the cross. And we acknowledge that it deserves every veneration. The image of a suffering man is applied to the cross so that the passion of Jesus Christ which brings salvation is renewed for us. Embrace it humbly! As a suppliant venerate it! And you shall recall these things to your memory. Moreover, you, O good Jesus, who while hanging for me on the cross suffered so, deign to be merciful. And show thyself, as the one who has died for me, and has died for this reason: that dying to this world I might live in you, O good Jesus. Thus also St Jerome encourages Eustochium to make the sign of the cross at each step. And St Ambrose, in his sermon on the cross, exhorts us to look always upon Christ, who freed us from death.

It would be tedious to recount how God with his astonishing power punished those who had profaned his sacred images. The extraordinary event which took place at Mainz, when a most wretched adventurer violated the image of the crucifix, must suffice for us Germans. Teodoricus Gresmundus vividly described this in a poem. Also well known in the court of Zolren of the diocese of Constance is the story of the archer who, persuaded by the Devil, shot an arrow into an image of the Saviour, from which blood immediately flowed. Thus if God when angered does not punish the iconoclasts right away, yet evil men should reflect on what is said in the old proverb: The vengeance of God comes noiselessly. And also on what Valerius Maximus says: Divine wrath moves at a slow pace to vengeance, and compensates for that by the severity of the punishment.

## Chapter V. The use of images is rational because it instructs the laity and refers them to the saints.

So far it has been sufficiently demonstrated that images were always used by the Church. Now a methodical approach requires us to explain that the use of images is in accord with reason and is useful and quite necessary. In the first place, it appears to us that the use of images for common people and illiterate is almost indispensable. For truly, as John of Damascus said: Since not all know how to read nor incline towards reading, our Fathers agreed to represent some things with images, as if they were memorials of some sort, to prompt the memory. And this is what is commonly said: Pictures are the Scripture of laity. Pope Gregory set out this reason to Serenus,[14] bishop of

---

[14] Original has Servius; the error is repeated below, see note 28. Again, this

Marseilles, saying: What Scripture presents to those who are literate, the picture provides to the illiterate who gaze upon it. Because the ignorant see in it the actions that have to be imitated; in it they who do not know letters are able to read. And thus, especially for the common people, pictures take the place of reading. And I do not know how the vast multitude of simple people can be better instructed in the sacred mysteries of our faith—nor how they can keep them more firmly in their minds—than through the use of images. This one reason ought to suffice and is why the holy Church adopted the use of images.[15]

Then John of Damascus adduces another reason from St Basil, since Basil, great in divine wisdom and one who carries the Word of God, says that the honour shown to the image is conveyed to what the image represents. For this reason the cult and the respect shown to the images of the saints and the crucifix are transferred to the crucified Christ and to the saints just as though to the prototypes and originals of the image. By virtue of this, John of Damascus says that the people of Moses worshipped the tabernacle in an indirect way, as something which was the image and shape of heavenly things. It is for this reason that God said to Moses: See to it that all things be done according to the form exhibited to you on the mountain. This relationship between the image and what it represents has been established so that the use of images makes people pure and whole, as we shall explain more fully at the end, when we deal with objections. Therefore, just as according to the first argument the laity are instructed by images, so by the second they are taught to refer every impulse of the soul to what is represented so they do not vainly bestir themselves over images.[16]

### Chapter VI. The use of images is rational because images help those who look upon them to remember.

And the use of images also causes the memory and recollection of Christ and the saints to arise more frequently and to be more firmly

---

passage on the *Biblia pauperum* might have been inspired by John of Damascus (see his commentary to the first oration, tr. Anderson, 38ff.), who mentions Basil.

[15] On Pope Gregory and the Bible of the illiterate, see Introduction, note 18.

[16] Again, the idea of the prototype, which goes back to Basil, could be found expressed in John of Damascus' first oration, ch. 21 (tr. Anderson, 29). The concept is repeated in ch. XVI below.

imprinted in the mind. Thus the triumphal sign of the cross, the images of the Virgin Mary or other saints are put in churches and public buildings to move the minds of the faithful, when they look upon them, to remember the mystery of redemption. Therefore, it follows logically that not only do images teach the laity, as they in truth do, but admonish and, as it were, importune, since they are not merely the likenesses of things but move and impel those who see them to pray or to do something.

For truly, how few of the faithful are there, who when passing an image of the holy Virgin as they go along are not stimulated to offer to her, who now rejoices in heaven with her Son, a pious greeting? Or if someone sees the image of the crucifix, does not the most bitter suffering of Christ come to mind? It is as that saying of Jeremiah in the Lamentations [1:12]: All of you who pass by, look upon me and see if there is a sorrow like my sorrow. Who, when seeing his image and the manifestation of such a great mystery, will be so hard and so ungrateful as not to give thanks to our Saviour for the mystery of redemption, especially since Christ requires from the Christian nothing other than a constant remembrance of his passion? (St Bernard, St Anselm, among others, have piously and diligently written much on this issue.) Therefore, whoever tries to remove images strives for nothing other than to weaken the memory of the passion of Christ and of his saints. No Christian ignores that such is the work of the Devil. There is no need to waste more words on something so clear. On the other hand, we can show from philosophy and rhetoric that memory benefits greatly from images.

## Chapter VII. Images are praiseworthy because they challenge the faithful to imitation.

There is another reason for the defence of images to which one cannot object. They invite and challenge the faithful to live chastely, piously, and in a truly Christian way in imitation of what they see. In just the same way, the ancients, in accord with the sound traditions of the republic, represented the illustrious deeds of their heroes and courageous men in marble statues, on columns, in paintings, and in poems so as not to seem ungrateful and to stimulate subsequent generations, by means of these sharp reminders, to eagerly imitate their deeds by emulating them. The same [has been] done in that very great nation of Christ which is the Church of God. John of Damascus says: We set up statues to the saints and visible images so that we ourselves through the imitation of [their] virtues may be turned into living statues and images of them. The same John of Damascus says in another passage: In a similar way also the great deeds of the saints prepare us to strength and zeal, to the imitation of their virtues, and finally to the glory of God. The Egyptians, the Assyrians, the Persians, the Greeks, the Romans, the Germans, and now also the Venetians were so grateful to the well-deserving men of the republic that they dedicated statues to their posterity. Why should we Christians be less grateful to those more-than-heroic men, God's saints? For the honour which is shown to the kind and gracious fellow-servants is the sign of goodwill toward a common god. If there were time, I could speak at length about the kinds of virtues and tell, one after the other, many memorable stories of the saints which would surpass by far the illustrious deeds of the Greek and Roman heroes. But I do not want to speak too much about what is obvious, since the remedies for all sins are found by pondering on the suffering of Christ alone.

**Chapter VIII. The use of images increases devotion.**
Now, I would think that the best known reason for the use of images is that not only do they recall to us the memory of Christ and the saints, and elevate the faithful by inviting them to imitate the saints, but also because they stimulate a feeling of devotion. For the mind itself is more powerfully moved and set afire by the lower senses and by tangible signs. Augustine affirms this in Book 2 of *On Visiting the Ill*. There are certain external signs which sometimes stimulate even those of sluggish faith, causing a kind of pang of conscience deep within them. The Christian religion requires these signs to be observed; and the devotion of friends gathered around the ill rejoices in their fulfillment.

The Venerable Bede also attests to this: No word of divine Scripture forbids images. Indeed, their appearance occasions much remorse for those looking upon them, and for those who are illiterate, they manifest something like a living record of the passion of Christ. The pagans write marvelous things about images capable of moving the minds of men. What, then, is wanting in images of the crucifix, of Mary, and of the saints, that they too may not move human emotions and stimulate the powers of the mind to celestial and divine matters? Who could express the great spiritual devotion which St Bernard repeatedly experienced before the image of Christ on the cross? Or who could adequately imagine the ardent desire and spiritual fire of St Francis' whole being when he embraced the image of Christ with such power of his imagination? He burned with such a great fire that he was endowed by him with the likeness of the stigmata of his passion.

There are thousands of examples like these recorded everywhere in histories and ecclesiastical writings. From all this it is clear to everyone how much the use of images has contributed to the Church of God. Useful contributions. Those who falsely believe that images must be destroyed, on the contrary, want trouble and harm in the Church of God, namely ignorance among the laity, forgetfulness in general, and laziness and lack of interest in life. Especially in these times, when the love of many has cooled, there must be aids and encouragements to devotion.

The old defences and aids should not be removed. But an evil man wants to sow the fields of the Lord with weeds. Now this advice could only come from the Devil, who laments over the fruits which come forth from the use of images, and who fears and flees images of the crucifix and the saints, as the story of St Christopher makes clear.

## Chapter IX. Regarding those who have opposed images.[17]
Although now, by reason of what has been said and carefully examined, I do not believe the faithful doubt that use of images—a custom which traces its origins to Christ himself, our Saviour—is good, productive, and well-nigh necessary; nevertheless, to avoid anger and injury, it is a good thing to know when and by whom the Church was plagued by most desperate men regarding the use of images. John of Damascus, who lived close to the time of the early martyrs of the Church—about 390[18]—records that from the beginning the faithful were reproached because they worshipped and venerated the images of our Saviour, of the Queen who gave birth to God, and those of other saints and servants of Christ. It appears [to us] that at the very time when the persecutions of the tyrants ceased and altars were being publicly erected and decorated, the demon wanted to stop the use and veneration of images (as something harmful to him, however beneficial it was for the faithful),

---

[17] Original has "quibus imaginibus fuerint adversati." Since the content of the chapter is on the iconoclasts, it would appear that the original should have been "qui imaginibus fuerint adversati."

[18] Eck's dates are incorrect; John of Damascus lived between c. 675 and 749.

though there are not lacking those who think that around the beginning of the law of the Gospels, men were found who condemned the veneration of images as a superstition and something approaching idolatry.

And still, after the glorious struggles of the martyrs and the frequent outbursts of heresy down to our own times, the impiety has often raged in the Church. For Philippicos, who seized the supreme power after the emperors Justinian and Tiberius had been slain, was led astray by the heretical monk John and disgracefully scraped away the images of the saints from the walls of St Sophia. Leo followed not long after him. He had a disagreement with the pope and sought an opportunity to injure him. Led astray by a wicked man, he issued an edict that everyone who lived in the Roman Empire should remove and carry away from the churches all the statues and images of saints, angels, and martyrs. He gathered them—even including images of the Saviour and Mary—in the middle of the city and burned them. Anyone opposing the edict was considered an impious enemy. And since many of the people did not consent to this foolish impiety, they were beheaded. Also, the patriarch Germanos, who had opposed this error, was expelled and Anastasius was chosen to replace him.[19]

After it had been suspended for a little while, Leo renewed the decree, ordered that all images—whether wood, bronze or marble—be brought to him and burned them. Those who did bring the images to him, he seized and put to the sword. To the impious father succeeded a worse son, the emperor Constantine, who destroyed holy images everywhere. The patriarch Constantine, who opposed his ungodliness, he put to death by flogging and replaced him with the eunuch Niceta, who had taken part in his sacrilege. And because Sabinus, king of the Bulgarians, followed him in the ungodly destruction of images, he ceased hostilities against him, reconciling himself

---

[19] Philippicos was emperor between 711 and 713 and succeeded Tiberius III and Justinian II. Other emperors quoted in the narrative are: Leo III (717–741), Constantine V (741–775), Leo IV (775–780), Constantine VI (780–797). The following emperors reigned between 797 and 820: Irene, Nikephoros, Staurakios, Michael I Rhangabe, and Leo V.

The story of the iconoclasm is taken from Theophanes' *Chronicle* (see Select Bibliography). For a modern history of the iconoclasm, Martin, *A History*; a recent survey of the controversy with some original texts translated into English can be found in Sahas, *Icon and Logos*.

with a man against whom he had previously waged war. Constantine's Propraetor Eunuchus, who administered the province of Thrace, a man even harsher than the emperor, was diligent in taking down and burning images of the crucifix and the saints. And after he sold all the ornaments of the churches at auction, he sent the money to the emperor. Constantine praised him highly in letters as a man after his own heart.

Selecting from men of his own kind, the impious emperor convened a synod of 330 bishops, which he wanted to call the Seventh Ecumenical Council.[20] However, it was only called the 'Constantinian Council.' It decreed that images, statues, and paintings of saints were to be removed from the churches. Leo, the heir of his father's empire and impiety, ordered the remaining images to be destroyed and condemned to death anyone who made a new image. He plundered the sanctuary of St Sophia and with gems taken from everywhere made a crown of great weight. His son, Constantine, equalled or surpassed the impiety of his great-grandfather, grandfather, and father. He blasphemed God and the saints and was irreverent towards his mother. The evil iconoclasm continued under the emperors Nicephorus, Staurakius, Michael, and Leo the Armenian, although it did not rate so much as under the previous four and was mitigated during the reign of the empress Irene, a most pious woman.

During the time that Charlemagne held the reins of the empire the plague also crept into Germany through an unhappy man by the name of Felix, after whom the Felician heresy is called. The emperor Michael in Constantinople sent representatives to the emperor Lothar in Rouen to discuss what should be done about images and judge whether or not they had to be abolished or restored to use.

## Chapter X. The Roman popes restored the images abolished by the emperors.

We have given a step by step account of the evil men who strove to overthrow and completely eradicate the use and cult of images. And the holy Fathers defended images just as strenuously as the heretics attacked them. For when first the emperor Philippicos destroyed images, Pope Constantine, in a council of bishops summoned to the

---

[20] The iconoclastic Council of Hieria, of 754. The decisions of this council were rejected and condemned by the second Council of Nicea in 787.

Lateran to deal with the issue, condemned the views of Philippicos and the monk John as foreign to the faith. And there, in the portico of St Peter, where the error regarding images was rejected, the pope had painted the images of the holy Fathers who had taken part in the six official councils of Constantinople. In the same council the pope decreed that the name of the heretical emperor should not be used in either public or private inscriptions in bronze, silver, or lead. The vengeance of God carried out this judgement of the pope against the sacrilegious emperor, for in the second year of his reign Philippicos was deprived of both power and his eyes by Anastasios, who promised to the pope that he would follow the doctrine of the sixth synod and of the Roman church.[21]

Gregory II, the younger of this name, not only refused to obey the command of the emperor, but also admonished all Catholics not to tumble into such great error out of fear, respect for the edict of princes, or for any other reason. The people of Italy were so aroused by this exhortation that they very nearly chose another emperor for themselves. But Gregory, by means of his authority, prevented this from happening. And in Ravenna civil strive erupted over the issue of whether the emperor or the pope was to be obeyed. In this uprising the governor Paul and his son were killed. Despite this calamity, the emperor did not desist from his impiety, but, on the contrary, in a new edict continued to insist that images be removed and burned.

The good pope called another council of holy Fathers (following in the footsteps of his predecessor) and once again condemned the heresy which called for the removal of images. He also deprived the sacrilegious patriarch Anastasios of his chair and removed him from his religious duties until he should revert to the Catholic faith. Frequently thereafter, as befitted that most holy man, he admonished the emperor in letters to dismiss the errors of certain wicked men and embrace the true faith. He also admonished him to stop doing away with images of the saints, whose memory and deeds inspire men to virtue and imitation. But he was speaking to deaf ears.

And so that you do not believe that I have made these things up, I want you to know, good reader, that the things which pertain to

---

[21] The popes mentioned in this chapter are Constantine (708–715), Gregory II (715–731), Gregory III (731–741), Stephen III (768–772), Hadrian I (772–795), and Leo III (795–816).

the history of popes were taken, for the most part verbatim, from Platina's *Lives of the Popes*,[22] [in those cases] when I knew that other chroniclers agree with him in all respects. But if he omitted something, I have most carefully added it, where it fits our purpose, by faithfully drawing upon other sources, because I seek nothing here other than the glory of God and the veneration due to the saints.

### Chapter XI. The use of images was the occasion for transferring the empire to the Germans.

The next step in our argument requires us to remind our Germany (remember, O Germany, what is excellent and fitting) that the most powerful reason for transferring the empire from the Greeks to the Germans was the use of images, which the sacrilegious emperors of Greece with such great malice, impiety, and sacrilege strove to remove and extirpate. This issue began to be discussed under Gregory II and continued to be discussed for nearly ninety years, to the time of Pope Leo III. Therefore, do not forget, O Germany, the honour you received and give thanks to the Church and especially to God. Then scatter and exterminate, just as if they were beings rejected by God and enemies of the fatherland, those sacrilegious men of Belial, infelicitous followers of Felix, who both counsel and preach that images must be removed. Do this, so that what in earlier times was the cause of your receiving the empire does not also become the cause of losing both glory and empire. God is not to be mocked; sacrilegious inventions of these kinds have never had good results.

But let us return to the subject at hand. The impious emperor Leo did not acquiesce to the most salutary admonitions of Gregory II. When Gregory II died, Gregory III succeeded him in the pontificate. From the first he made a great effort (although in vain) to recall the emperors Leo and his son Constantine to the observance of the true faith and effect the restitution of images. Finally, he convoked a council in the church of St Peter's and decreed that images should not be abolished but should be honoured with veneration, in accord with the decrees of the councils of his predecessors Constantine and Gregory II. And he also deposed and excommunicated the sacrilegious emperor Leo.

---

[22] See Emser, note 24. On Platina as a source for Eck, see Iserloh, "Die Verteidigung," 82.

And let the Germans know, so that they might better appreciate these Gregories, that it was they who sent the martyr Boniface to Germany as a legate of the Holy See. He converted idolaters (of whom there were then a great number in Germany) to the Christian faith and was crowned with martyrdom by the pagan Frisians. He raised Mainz to an archiepiscopal seat (before it was part of Worms), instituted the bishoprics of Würzburg and Eistetten, and divided Bavaria into the four parishes (as they were called by Pope Gregory) of Salzburg, Passau, Regensburg, and Freising. For these reasons Boniface, the legate of the Gregories, is deservedly called by everyone the apostle of the Germans.

Now at that time the pontiffs favoured the Germans and it happened under Gregory III that for the first time the defence of the Church was transferred from the emperors in Constantinople to the German Franks. For while Luitprand, king of the Lombards, immoderately waged war on the papacy, for the reasons relating to images which we have mentioned the pope did not want to seek help from the emperor in Constantinople, as up that time the Church was accustomed to do. Therefore, the pope turned to Charles Martel,[23] grandfather of Charlemagne, and through legates asked him to come to the aid of Rome and Church. Charles did so with vigour. Thus also, Pope Stephen implored Pepin, the son of Charles Martel, for aid against Astiulphus. Thus, again, Stephen III, Hadrian I, and Leo III drew upon the services and aid of Charles, son of Pepin, to protect the Church and spurned the sacrilegious emperors in Constantinople.

Finally, with the assent of the clergy and people of Rome, Pope Leo transferred the empire to Charlemagne of Germany, and it remains with the Germans to this day. Thus, because the sacrilegious emperor Leo abolished, eradicated, and demolished images, God took the Roman Empire from him and his successors.

## Chapter XII. The evil things that happened to the emperors who removed images.

The sacrilegious tyrants who followed Leo suffered similar harm when, like the giants, they attempted to cast God down from heaven, by abolishing images of the crucifix and the saints. Pope Paul I sent

---

[23] Original has Marcellum.

ambassadors to Constantinople to persuade Constantine V that he
should restore sacred images and statues, so as not to imitate the
sacrilege of his father. He threatened him with excommunication if
he should refuse, and afterwards did publicly excommunicate the
stubborn emperor. The fact that Sabinos, king of the Bulgars, had
followed Constantine's impiety was so hard for the Bulgarians to
accept regarding their king that they had in mind to kill him; but he
sought safety at Constantinople by flight.

Also Pope Stephen III, after a council held in the Lateran, which
had been organized by Charlemagne and other Christian princes to
discuss the matter with many bishops, abrogated the Constantinian
Council of Constantinople (which the sacrilegious dared to call the
Seventh Synod). And by general agreement of the Fathers, it was
decreed that images and statues should be everywhere restored and
that those who had presided over the Constantinian Synod should
be excommunicated together with the emperor because they
believed the condition of God was worse than that of men to whom
statues are erected in memory of their good deeds. The tyrant
scorned the healing medicine of excommunication and for his crimes
God began already in this world to torment him with plagues. He
began to suffer heavily from elephantiasis. Through this disease, due
the weakness of the brown and foamy blood, his putrid flesh, peeling
from his sinews and bones, brought him, covered with ulcers, to an
end which was most cruel but also best suited to his whole life.[24]

This also happened to his son Leo, the heir of his impiety. At first
he simulated true religious devotion and was much loved by his
subjects. But when he began to imitate the crimes of his father and
stripped the sanctuary of St Sophia of gold, jewels, and all precious
things, divine vengeance immediately followed and he was carried
off by sudden death. When Leo died, Irene, a most religious empress
who opposed the decrees of the most impious emperors, took up
the reins of government together with her son Constantine. She first
restored religious rites and observances by summoning a council of
350 Catholic bishops to Nicea, where it was appropriately established
that whoever declared that the images of saints must be destroyed

---

[24] Here Eck elaborates on a much less detailed description by Theophanes (the
death of Constantine V in 775 and Leo IV in 741 are described at pp. 135 and 139f.
of the edition quoted). Divine revenge against the iconoclasts is a pervasive *topos*
throughout Theophanes' *Chronicle*.

should be permanently excommunicated. And the Constantinian Synod was condemned there. The very next year she called the same Fathers to Constantinople and she wanted that synod, and not the Constantinian one, to be called the Seventh Ecumenical Council. There are, however, those who believe that that synod was declared the Seventh [Ecumenical Council] under Pope Eugene II when Michael was the emperor in Constantinople.

## Chapter XIII. The heresies of Felix of Urgel regarding images were condemned in Frankfurt during the reign of Charlemagne.

But her son Constantine, the sixth of that name, adopted the advice of wicked men and annulled the very salutary decrees of the council. Pushing aside his mother, he assumed sole rule of the empire and took pleasure in the blinding and slaying of many men. But Irene, his mother, would not tolerate his crimes and, impelled by the nobility of her character, had her son seized, blinded, and thrown into prison, where he suffered the just punishment of his impiety and sacrilege. And Irene restored images.

In the same way, the heresy of Felix was extinguished almost as soon as it began through the efforts of Pope Hadrian and Charlemagne. For when Charlemagne was subduing the Hungarians because of their almost daily raids, he came with his nobles to the eastern portion of his realm (where the Franks originated) in Germany, and there, in the year of our Lord 793 summoned a synod of French and German bishops to congregate in Frankfurt, over which presided Bishops Theophilatius and Stephen, legates of the Holy See. It condemned the heresy of Felix and forbade anyone, under threat of excommunication, to destroy images or teach that they should be abolished.[25] Hence the pestilential disease developed no further for 730 years. But now, in the year of our Lord 1522—if the story is true—the heresy of Felix is spreading out once again from the north. Luther, Karlstadt, and Melanchthon—men cut off from the Church of God—are its authors. But it is our best hope that he who overthrew with punishments and torments the sacrilegious men who destroyed

---

[25] On the condemnation of the Spanish bishop Felix of Urgel and Eck's narrative, see Iserloh, "Die Verteidigung," 81; contrary to what Iserloh states, however, Eck knew the *Libri Carolini*: see N. Harpsfeld, *Dialogi* (Antwerp, 1566), 563 and 594f.

images of the saints [will not allow][26] these iconoclasts to escape the just punishment for their impiety and sacrilege. And just as the most Christian prince Charlemagne repressed the heresy of Felix and converted the Saxons to the faith, so now our glorious caesar Charles [V], the Catholic king, shall cut back the reborn heresy and shall prevent the Saxons from abandoning the faith.

The spokesmen whom Michael sent to the emperor Lothar, Lothar sent to the Apostolic See, which rules in all matters concerning faith. There they were instructed by Eugene II that the heresy of abolishing images of Christ and of the saints had been condemned by five councils—three in Rome, one in Nicea, and another in Frankfurt—and he exhorted them to persuade the emperor to restore images.

**Chapter XIV. The decrees against those who remove images.**
Gregory II[27] severely rebuked Serenus,[28] bishop of Marseilles, because he had destroyed some images. He wrote to him and said: It has been reported to us that inflamed by an inconsiderate zeal you have destroyed some images of the saints on the grounds that they should not be worshipped. That you have forbidden them to be worshipped we certainly praise. But we disapprove of your destroying them. Tell us, brother, if you have ever heard that a priest did what you have done. For it is one thing to worship a painting; it is another thing to learn from the story the pictures tells what is to be worshipped.

For this reason, in the Seventh Synod (not that one called the Constantinian) the oath regarding the destruction of images, seeing that it concerned something illegal, was in part useless. For we read in the acts of the fourth session of the Seventh Synod that John, a delegate from the east, said: The speech of our Father Sophronios signifies that it would be better for the oath-taker to commit perjury than to keep his oath for the breaking of sacred images. And we say that because certain people are excusing themselves from this oath. The patriarch Tarasios said that since Father Sophronios knew the

---

[26] The text of this sentence is corrupt and the verb is missing.

[27] Eck here confuses Gregory I, pope from 590 to 604, whose famous letter to Serenus he quotes, and Gregory II, 715–731. For the letter by Gregory I (the Great) on images, see Introduction, note 18.

[28] Servius in the original: see above, note 14.

goodness of God, for that reason he wanted to violate the impious oath.[29]

Here it is clear that before the time of Gregory no priest did what our sacrilegious men Luther and Karlstadt are endeavouring to do. It is also clear that the synod judged the removal of images to be illegal, and that even if an oath has been taken to do so, it ought not to be observed. But our headless cynic and epicurean theologians are striving with all their strength to do this, even though they have not taken an oath.

I find in this regard one ruling of the Synod of Constantinople which reads as follows: We decree that the holy images of our Lord Jesus Christ, Deliverer and Saviour of all, be adored with the same honour as the book of the holy Gospels. And further on it says: Therefore, if someone does not worship the icon of Christ the Saviour, let him not see his form when he comes to be glorified in the glory of his Father and to glorify his saints, but let him be kept away from his communion and his light. Now, may Luther and his fellows in crime see what sort of anathema strikes them. But, as John said [Rev. 22:11]: And he which is filthy, let him be filthy still.[30]

## Chapter XV. The fallacious reasons advanced by the iconoclasts.

Now that we have secured our positions, it remains for us to break the strength of our adversaries and undermine their foundations. It appears they have five main grounds for taking the opportunity to commit such crime and impiety. The first is that it is in Exodus 20[:4ff.], where God's commandments are given, that images are prohibited. The text says: Thou shalt not make unto thee any graven image or any likeness of anything that is in heaven above, or that is in the earth beneath, or that is in the water under the earth.[31] The

---

[29] Note on the margin: "Non habeo iam ad manum acta illa synodorum quia plures volunt illa tractata in vi synodo. Hoc tantum verissimum: quod Tharasius vii synodo catholice interfuit." The acts of the fourth session of Nicea II are in G.D. Mansi, *Conciliorum Collectio*, vol. 13 (Florence, 1767), 1–156; the section referring to the oath, ibid., 62ff.

[30] The acts of this council, which convened in the years 869–870, are also in Mansi's *Conciliorum Collectio*, vol. 16 (Florence, 1767), 1–534; the section quoted by Eck, ibid., 161–162.

[31] On the Decalogue, see Karlstadt, notes 8 and 22.

second is that Scripture praises King Hezekiah by saying that afterwards there was no king in Judah like him. And it was he who threw down the hill-shrines, smashed statues, cut down the sacred groves, and also broke the brazen serpent which Moses had made (2 Kings 18[:4]), although God himself ordered it to be made (Num. 21[:8]).[32] To these passages must be added what the Saviour said to the woman of Samaria (John 4[:21–23]): Believe me, the time is coming when you will worship the Father neither on this mountain, nor in Jerusalem. You Samaritans worship without knowing what you worship; we worship what we know. It is from the Jews that salvation comes. But the time approaches, indeed it is already here, when those who are worshippers will worship in spirit and in truth,[33] for the Father seeks such to worship him. God is a spirit: and they that worship him must worship him in spirit and truth.

Moreover, many troublesome and serious dangers seem to arise from the use of images. When a man thinks too much about images and the corporeal things around him, not only might he be touched by idolatry, but also, because of the wavering of his fantasy and the mocking cooperation of the invisible enemy, he might turn from devotions and pious thoughts to thinking impure and obscene things. That is to say, he may turn from spiritual matters to corporeal and carnal things. For danger can easily threaten those who have too much contact with the image of nude saints. Who can doubt the possibility that someone while meditating might cling so intensely to the crucifix that the crucified Lord disappears and he remains alone together with the two thieves? Thus also a shameful and indecent picture of holy virgins may lead to abominable thoughts.

Finally, a certain good, learned man (whose name, out of respect, I do no mention, as he would definitely wish)[34] perhaps unaware that this matter had formerly been so often defined by [ecclesiastical] councils, discusses at great length this question concerning the removal of images. First, he says that images are prohibited by the inviolable Ten Commandments, although he dilutes that objection

---

[32] On Hezekiah, see Karlstadt, note 15.

[33] In referring to John 4:21–23, Eck contradicts Karlstadt and other Reformers who held that this passage condemned any cult of a physical object.

[34] The unnamed man whose views are discussed in this passage must be Paulus Ricius, the convert from Judaism, whose discussion of the Mosaic Law is also mentioned and rejected by Emser. See Emser, note 8.

of the Jews. Again he insists that not only must one guard against the execrable crime of idolatry, but also against whatever might pollute the conscience of simple folk, such as the pestiferous and shameful adoration of images which immediately drives away all the care and protection of God. Finally, he rejected the reasons offered by ecclesiastical writers in defence of images, especially those of St Thomas Aquinas, on the grounds that this kind of cult of images was established by none of the apostles nor by any canonical ruling. On the contrary, it is rejected with the highest contempt and accusation, according to that which the apostle says: And they changed the glory of the uncorruptible God into an image made like to corruptible man [Rom. 1:23]; or again: Flee from idolatry [1 Cor. 10:14], that is from images. From this it follows that because it proceeds from the permission of images and it leads to eternal ruin, the suspicion of idolatry is worse than the results of ignorance, forgetfulness, and lukewarm devotion. Therefore, he concludes by saying that the corrupt seed of an unhealthy custom generated the use of images in the Christian community (like the seeds of wild grape in the vineyard or of darnels in the most carefully cultivated field of wheat). Furthermore, he believes that it was impossible to eradicate the use of images from the heathens who were used to the simulacra because the crazy and torpid mass of those people preferred to forget the pious religion of Christ rather than the vain veneration of simulacra.

This is finally his conclusion: But I nevertheless, with all due deliberation, dare to declare this one thing, that since the orthodox faith of Christ has now been restored to fullness, it would not be harmful (save only it would involve struggling against the excesses of a long established custom), but on the contrary, proper and laudable, to build churches and chapels stripped of statues of the saints. Indeed, this, and not physical images made by hand, would raise the minds of men to the elevated and ethereal spirits of the saints. And also it would save the weak from temptation.

**Chapter XVI. The first argument is dismissed and the reason for venerating images explained.**

In the first place, it is clear—if these matters are judged correctly—that it is the abuse of images, rather than images themselves, that is prohibited. For God, in Exodus, does not simply prohibit sculptures and images, but, rather, forbids the making of statues to which a divine cult is offered in the manner of the idolaters. For after the passage just mentioned, the text continues: You shall not bow down to them nor worship them. Here we touch upon the decisive reason, and that this is so is made clear in the immediately following chapter (Exodus 25) when God orders images of the cherubim to be made. Thus God did not want the people, who were otherwise prone to idolatry, to make frequent use of images, so that they would not fall into the vain practices of the pagans, as did happen on other occasions.

But now, in the period under the Law of Grace, when men are no longer so inclined to idolatry, no such danger exists. And the reason justifying the use of images, in such a way that they can pose no danger to the laity, is simple and singular, and that is, according to the great Basil, that the cult, veneration, and respect shown to an image does not go to the image itself but to the archetype; to that which is represented. Therefore, God prohibited images because the people were inclined to idolatry, and yet the priests, whom we may not presume to be so inclined, had images of the angelic cherubim in the Holy of Holies, so that by looking upon them and contemplating the celestial order the mind of the high priest would be elevated.

John of Damascus offers this elegant explanation. Just as the Jews and Greeks sacrificed in different ways, so there are differences between pagan and Christian images. Pagan images, in which the foolish pagans believed divinity lurked, were dwelling places of demons. Christian images are representations of Christ, of Mary, and of the saints. For just as we do not worship the material with which the Gospels are written, neither do we worship the material from which the cross is made, but rather what the type and figure express. Therefore, Christians observe the intention of the Law and Law-giver since they use images as instructors, counsellors, and as things which awaken interest and not as things which have a divinity hidden within them.

St Augustine, in Book 3, chapters 7 and 8 of *Christian Instruction*, also attributes this kind of difference to signs. The Church rejected the useless representations of the Gentile gods and accepted the images of Christ and the saints, and the signs of the sacraments related to God and the saints.

And it seems to me that St Augustine rendered pious and learned judgements on this issue in Book 22 of *The City of God*. While the cult of idols will be thrown to the city of the Devil, he teaches that martyrs are rightly venerated because of the many miracles they received from God, to the end that the true God is worshipped. And I cannot entirely pass over in silence two passages in the same work. One is what he says about the miracles of the saints. The martyrs perform them, or rather God does, either in answer to their prayers or using them as co-workers, to advance the faith. We do not believe the martyrs to be our gods, but rather than we and they have one God. The other is when he says: We do not build temples to our martyrs as if to gods, but as memorials to dead men whose spirits are with the living God. Nor do we erect altars in them on which sacrifice to the martyrs, but we offer a sacrifice to one God, the martyrs' and ours. They are named in a particular part of that sacrifice as men of God who conquered the world in confessing him, but the priest who makes the sacrifice does not call upon them. For in fact he sacrifices to God and not to them, even if he sacrifices in their memory, since he is God's priest and not theirs.

It seems proper to cite these most vigorous words of the holy Father St Augustine, as learned as he was saintly, because he teaches us not only in what manner images of the saints should be venerated, but also [how] the saints themselves should be. For whatever problem Augustine touched upon, he solved wisely and prudently, although some, considering all things, place Jerome many steps before him.

Thus the meaning of the declaration of the synod is clear (whether it was the sixth or seventh does not matter, so long as it is understood that it was not the one called the Constantinian Synod). It says: Christians do not call venerable images gods, nor do they serve them as gods; nor place hope of salvation in them; nor expect a future judgement from them. We venerate and worship them in memory and recollection of the early martyrs, but we do not serve them or any other created thing with a divine cult.[35]

So now we understand in what sense we ought not to make a graven image, and that is to worship and adore it as a god.

---

[35] Eck wants to avoid confusion between the two councils, one of which he considers invalid: see above, note 20. The 'declaration' reported by Eck can be found in the acts of Nicea (second) of 787: see Sahas, *Icon and Logos*, 64.

**Chapter XVII. Reflections on the brazen serpent, and also an argument that the fact that we ought to worship in spirit and truth does not abolish images.**

Whatever can be said about the brazen serpent is certainly not against the use of images; on the contrary, it strongly confirms it. For although in Exodus the Lord prohibited graven images, nevertheless soon after, in Numbers 21, the Lord said to Moses: Make a serpent of bronze and set it as a sign, so that everyone who is bitten, when he looks upon it, shall live (Num. 21[:8]). Thus God, in this passage, ordered a graven image to be made, but this was to be understood as a sign or to be destroyed, as the text clearly explains. Because the people, who were greatly inclined to idolatry, later took the serpent not as a sign, but worshipped it as a god, Hezekiah rightly destroyed that which had been made by the command of God.

Now the Church steadfastly maintains the first custom, holding images to be signs and not gods and therefore continues to use images. But if somewhere people take an image to be a god and not merely a sign, it must be destroyed. For as Pope Stephen rightly concluded, if the ancients made things without blame which later generations turn into error and superstition of some kind, those things must be destroyed by their successors without delay and with great determination.

Similarly also, the word of the Saviour does not exclude images. For true worshippers, admonished or instructed as they are by images, still worship in spirit and in truth if the prayers go to the prototype, as has been established by St Basil. For wherever a man prays, he prays in spirit and in truth, especially in the period under the Law of Grace when both the prefigurations of Moses have been removed and the dark falsehoods of the pagans have been dispelled. So it was also with David when he said: Let my cry come before thee, O Lord; give me understanding according to thy word (Psalm 118/119[:169]). And it is no less true when he says: In thy fear will I worship toward thy holy temple (Psalm 5[:8]). So it was with Hezekiah as quoted in Isaiah: Remember now, O Lord, I beseech thee, how I have walked before thee in truth and with a perfect heart, and done that which is good in thy sight (Isaiah 38[:3]). So it was with St Paul: I will pray with the Spirit, and I will pray with understanding also; I will sing with the Spirit, and I will sing with the understanding also (1 Cor. 14[:15]).

Now certainly, whoever would want thus to exclude external images on account of the spirit, with equal reason should also include in this ban physical signs of the sacraments, all religious ceremonies, and even the text of Scripture together with all vocal prayer. Therefore it is clear that images do not prevent us from worshipping in spirit and truth, but, on the contrary, stimulate us to do so.

## Chapter XVIII. The other arguments against images are dismissed and a concluding statement is appended.

Here, without much difficulty, we can refute the fourth argument brought forward against images, which blames the extravagance of painters who sometimes create images which are too licentious. It also blames the improvidence of those who pray. But it is not the use of images itself, or looking at them that does this, as the argument assumes, but rather the worshipper who clings excessively to the image. This shackles his heart, as if it were bound with ropes, so that it is not borne upward, or is even dragged downward by impure thoughts. Therefore, the faithful man ought to use images only as a sign, so that through them he be instructed, admonished, and stimulated; and through them he be immediately lifted up in spirit to thoughts of God and the saints. But if he becomes more wayward because of the sign (as the argument assumes) then it is not surprising if the meaning of the sign is lost on him. Jean Gerson, the most Christian chancellor of the University of Paris, in his book, *On the Private Spiritual Exercises of Simple People*, demonstrates this with many examples, all of which could be used here.[36] But for the sake of brevity I will merely direct the zealous reader to that book.

From all this it follows that the faithful must worship in spirit and in truth, both with images and without images.

The good man we spoke of above must be judged according to the conclusions to which he bears witness. Because he refers everything to the judgement of the Church, with which he wishes to live, learn, and find rest, the errors must be given the best possible interpretation, although this was not his practice in argument against

---

[36] The work is today attributed to a follower of J. Gerson, *Œuvres complètes*, ed. Glorieux (Paris, 1960), vol. 1, 58. Gerson did write a short piece on indecent images, *Adversus lascivas imagines*, which, however does not deal with religious art.

me, upon whom he inflicted many insults. But let God have mercy on us and preserve us.

Therefore, in response to his first assumption—that it is necessary to guard against that which tempts the simple—I simply do not admit that images tempt the simple. For they can make use of images correctly by the single and simple insistence that images refer to what they represent. However, the worship of images is destructive if it is idolatrous, that is if it involves the belief that something like a divinity resides in the images, as we have explained at some length. Then he erroneously rejects the explanations of St Thomas Aquinas, to whom he normally defers, inasmuch as the use of images in the Church, as we explained earlier, was introduced by Christ and the apostles. The fact that he cites the apostle concerning images of idols does not stand in the way of images of the saints, for we have learned the difference between the pagan and Christian images from John of Damascus and St Augustine. Consequently, we do no accept his interpretation of the statement: Flee from idolatry, that is to say, from images, for not all images are idols (unless he is prepared to say the cherubim on the mercy seat are idols), even if all idols are images. Thus his fear of idolatry arising from images is groundless, unless perchance it might come from men of his race, the Jews. But since they are blind and obstinate, as he himself complains about them, so great a good coming from images ought not to be impeded because of the perverse interpretation of the Jews. For if they wanted to listen, the one right way which separates the use of images from idolatry would easily be pointed out to them. But they have ears and do not hear [Mark 8:18].

His surmise that the apostles were unable to tear the pagans away from the use of images is also false. He cannot prove this from any source and therefore it is easily disregarded. Moreover, the opposite can be said, as we have clearly demonstrated.

As to his advice, farewell to it. For it is not seemly to destroy with his new considerations what the Church determined in five councils with much discussion and mature deliberation, although I fully believe that he wrote with good intention and acknowledges himself to be an obedient son of the Church.

It is clear, therefore, that the use of images in the Church must not be abolished at all. For it has Christ and the apostles as its authors, and the approval of the entire Church in five councils, despite sacrilegious emperors who attacked it for a hundred years. We ought to maintain the use of images of the crucified Christ and the saints because they instruct us and frequently remind us of them. Because of this, the saints and chosen of God, through the mercy of the Father, remember us in their prayers and seek for us the rewards of their merits so that one day we may be made their fellow citizens. Praising the Lord forever, Amen.

This treatise by Eck was finished on the 8th of March 1522.

To the glory of God alone.

# Publications of the
# Centre for Reformation and Renaissance Studies

## Renaissance and Reformation Texts in Translation:

Lorenzo Valla. *The Profession of the Religious and Selections from The Falsely-Believed and Forged Donation of Constantine*. Trans. O.Z. Pugliese. 2nd ed. (1994), pp. 114

Giovanni Della Casa. *Galateo: A Renaissance Treatise on Manners*. Trans. K. Eisenbichler and K.R. Bartlett. 3rd ed. (1994), pp. 98

Bernardino Ochino. *Seven Dialogues*. Trans. R. Belladonna (1988), pp. 96

Nicholas of Cusa. *The Layman on Wisdom and The Mind*. Trans. M.L. Führer (1989), pp. 112

Andreas Karlstadt, Hieronymous Emser, Johannes Eck. *A Reformation Debate: Karlstadt, Emser, and Eck on Sacred Images*. Trans. B. Mangrum and G. Scavizzi, 2nd ed. (1998), pp. 125

*Whether Secular Government Has the Right to Wield the Sword in Matters of Faith: A Controversy in Nürnberg in 1530*. Trans. James M. Estes (1994), pp. 118

Jean Bodin. *On the Demon-Mania of Witches*. Abridged, trans. & ed. R.A. Scott and J.L. Pearl (1995), pp. 219

## Tudor and Stuart Texts:

James I. *The True Law of Free Monarchies and Basilikon Doron*. Ed. with an intro. by D. Fischlin and M. Fortier (1996), pp. 181

## Occasional Publications:

*Register of Sermons Preached at Paul's Cross (1534-1642)*. Comp. M. MacLure. Revised by P. Pauls and J.C.Boswell (1989), pp. 151

*Annotated Catalogue of Early Editions of Erasmus at the Centre for Reformation and Renaissance Studies, Toronto*. Comp. J. Glomski and E. Rummel (1994), pp. 153

**For additional information, contact:**
**CRRS Publications, Victoria University, Toronto, Ontario**
**M5S 1K7, CANADA**
**(416) 585-4484, fax (416) 585-4579,**
**e-mail crrs@chass.utoronto.ca**